The Prayer of Jehoshaphat

The Prayer of Jehoshaphat

SEEING BEYOND LIFE'S STORMS

INCLUDES STUDY GUIDE

STANLEY D. GALE

P&R
PUBLISHING
P.O. BOX 817 • PHILLIPSBURG • NEW JERSEY 08865-0817

Italics within Scripture quotations indicate emphasis added.

Page design by Lakeside Design Plus

Printed in the United States of America

Library of Congress Cataloging-in-Publication Data

Gale, Stanley D., 1953–

The prayer of Jehoshaphat : seeing beyond life's storms / Stanley D. Gale.

p. cm.

ISBN-13: 978-1-59638-062-2 (pbk.)

1. Bible. O.T. Chronicles, 2nd, XX, 6-12–Criticism, interpretation, etc. 2. Prayer–Biblical teaching. 3. Jehoshaphat, King of Judah. I. Title.

BS1345.6.P68G35 2007

248.4—dc22

2007014460

In memory of Ray Dillard,
who made the Old Testament come alive
for me in Christ,
and to all those godly, learned men and women
God uses in our lives

Contents

Acknowledgments 9
Preface 11
Introduction: The Prayer of Who? 15

1. Storm Clouds on the Horizon 21
A great multitude is coming against you.

2. Seeing beyond the Storm 29
Jehoshaphat was afraid and set his face to seek the LORD.

3. Sharpening Our Gaze on Glory 37
Are you not God in heaven?

4. Privileged Access 47
We will . . . cry out to you in our affliction, and you will hear and save.

5. Prevailing Prayer 57
We do not know what to do, but our eyes are on you.

6. Sand Bags of Promise 67
Thus says the LORD to you.

7. Standing Firm 77
Stand firm and see.

8. Stepping Out 85
Go out against them, and the LORD will be with you.

9. Courage of Faith 95
Believe . . . and you will be established.

10. Aftermath of Grace 103
That place has been called the Valley of Beracah.

Conclusion 111
Climax 119
2 Chronicles 20:1–30 (ESV) 125
Study Guide 129

Acknowledgments

I am deeply grateful for those who read the manuscript, gave feedback, and encouraged me in the value of this small book: Linda Gale, Florence Lu, and Dwight Dunn. Al Groves is among the readers but deserves special mention because his reading was not merely as a dispassionate observer but as one in the grip of great personal upheaval as he wrestled with diagnosed terminal cancer and all its ramifications for himself and his family. His expression of how meaningful and helpful the book was to him in that distress gave credence to the work beyond any academic assessment. I am appreciative to Mark McCaffrey for providing me a quiet place to write. Finally, I want to thank Marvin Padgett of P&R Publishing for his enthusiasm for the project and allowing me to share these insights with you.

Preface

What do you do when you are overwhelmed by the enormity of life? Situations of such magnitude besiege you that you don't know how you can possibly weather them, let alone overcome them. Those onslaughts tower over you to such a degree that not only is the circumstance huge, your weaknesses, limitations, frailties, and inabilities are magnified as well.

Your first response might be to run. But you can't run. It will overtake you. You can't escape your life and right now that circumstance is not only occupying your life, it is dominating it. It looms large. You see it from every perch you take in the terrain of your existence.

With fight out of the question and flight not an option, what's left? The answer that strikes you is prayer. Prayer is prominent in both life and literature. Hikers stranded by an avalanche, abandoned to the elements, reach out in prayer. Novelists, depicting what might be expected in life's severe adversity, describe the kidnapped couple turning to prayer. Prayer is a natural recourse for a divine resource.

The question is what do we pray? What words can we find other than, "help?" To whom do we pray? Can we actually expect an answer?

This book is about prayer, prayer in dire circumstance. It's about finding our voice when we are confronted by daunting situations that threaten to snow us under, maybe even threaten our very life. This book is also about what to pray, giving content and clarity to the voice we find, and seeing the omnipotent God who invites our prayer.

The Bible is replete with prayers. The psalms are prayers, songs for all seasons that give expression to the gamut of emotions and needs. They are generated from real life experiences and serve to give honest voice in times of tumult.

But the prayer I am commending in this book is a prayer that I discovered early on in my Christian life. I encountered it while reading through the Bible in a year, and it jumped from the page to me. Ever since, I have used this prayer as a framework for approaching my God and Father in my times of deepest distress and even despair. As a Christian friend I have been able to take fellow believers overwhelmed with life to this prayer and to the foundation of hope it brings.

Sometimes portions of Scripture take a good deal of contextualization and explanation in order to understand them well enough to apply to our lives. This prayer, however, is one of those that can be ripped from its context to find immediate service in our need. Listen to its heart:

> O our God, will you not execute judgment on them? For we are powerless against this great horde that is coming against us. We do not know what to do, but our eyes are on you.

While this prayer readily lifts the troubled spirit up to God Almighty, our approach in the pages that follow will be to explore something of the breadth and depth of its setting that we might appreciate its richness. We'll bring to bear the expanding contexts of the prayer's immediate framework, its broader base in the book of the Bible that contains it, and the ultimate context of God's compassion and provision in Jesus Christ.

May the Lord richly bless you and minister to you as he draws you into his everlasting, almighty arms and gives you voice in time of need.

Introduction: The Prayer of Who?

Who is Jehoshaphat? Perhaps the only time you've heard the name is in the expression, "Jumpin' Jehoshaphat." A search on the web will show that there is no certainty where that phrase comes from or exactly what it means. It seems to be just a fun-sounding exclamation, like "leaping lizards," or, as my grandfather was fond of saying, "Great Caesar's ghost." But Jehoshaphat was a real person of biblical proportions.

Jehoshaphat was a king of ancient Israel. He was the son of Asa and the fourth king of the southern kingdom of Judah, in the line of David. He reigned from 873–49 BC, almost twenty-five years. He was a good king. His name means "The LORD has judged." Jehoshaphat had great concern for the glory of God and for faithfulness to his righteous decrees. As was to be the case in a theocracy, Jehoshaphat recognized that God was the real king. Jehoshaphat's job was to rule under God, for God, and by God.

Jehoshaphat was a good king in that he honored God and respected his wishes. An assessment of him is found in 2 Chronicles 17:3–4:

> The LORD was with Jehoshaphat, because he walked in the earlier ways of his father David. He did not seek the Baals, but sought the God of his father and walked in his commandments.

Later we are told that he was "courageous in the ways of the LORD" (2 Chron. 17:6).

An example of Jehoshaphat's mindset and heart can be seen in an interaction with a king whose heart was not so inclined to the Lord, King Ahab. You can read the entire account in 2 Chronicles 18. The gist is that Ahab wanted to ally himself with Jehoshaphat, joining forces against a common foe. Before he would commit himself, Jehoshaphat insisted, "Inquire first for the word of the LORD." Ahab gathered four hundred so-called prophets, who with one accord predicted success and encouraged the joint undertaking. Jehoshaphat, however, wasn't impressed. "Is there not here a prophet of the LORD of whom we may inquire?" Jehoshaphat wasn't interested in numbers, but in truth. The four hundred were unanimous but Jehoshaphat wanted to hear from his God.

Such was the heart of Jehoshaphat. His obituary captured his life in these terms:

> He walked in the way of Asa his father and did not turn aside from it, doing what was right in the sight of the LORD. (2 Chron. 20:32)

It was from this heart for God, awareness of God, and concern for the honor of God that we see his prayer.

Against All Odds

A great multitude, a vast horde assembled together against Jehoshaphat and his army. At least three nations, united as a mighty army, advanced against him. Word came to Jehoshaphat that this juggernaut loomed ominously on the horizon, poised to wreak havoc, destruction, and devastation.

Jehoshaphat was a king, commander of an army of his own. But his forces were paltry, dwarfed by the formidable army coming against him. He was like a dog that had strayed onto the interstate, facing a wall of surging, unstoppable agents of destruction.

When Jehoshaphat heard the news, he was gripped in fear—and rightly so. What could he do? How could he stand? Should he fight? Should he flee? Should he just roll over?

But Jehoshaphat was not alone. True, he was a king, but his rule was not absolute. His was a subordinate rule.

The Sovereign Lord of creation was with him. Steeped in a close walk with God, Jehoshaphat's reflexive action was to seek his Lord, not as last resort but as first recourse.

And so Jehoshaphat turned to his Lord in the face of sure ruin and sore distress. What does he ask of God?

> O our God, will you not execute judgment on them? For we are powerless against this great horde that is coming against us. We do not know what to do, but our eyes are on you. (2 Chron. 20:12)

Jehoshaphat addresses him as the God he is, and then he lays before this God his plea in utter honesty and abject awareness.

Finding Your Voice in Distress

> O our God, will you not execute judgment on them? For we are powerless against this great horde that is coming against us. We do not know what to do, but our eyes are on you.

Can you relate to this prayer? Don't its words fit you well, as a tailor-made suit contoured to the form of your distress? Does its flow that drains you of self and amplifies your inability run with the current of your anguished heart?

In this prayer of Jehoshaphat, God gives us a prayer of the powerless. We find recorded in his Word a prayer by which we might prevail upon him. Sometimes, it's all we can find the ingenuity and strength to utter.

Moreover, this prayer is remarkable not only for what it says, but for what it does not say. That's all part of its profound simplicity.

Let's turn to this prayer of Jehoshaphat.[1] Let's delve into what our God has provided to give us voice in distress, despair, and disaster. Let's explore the anchor he gives us in time of storm. And, particularly, let us give ear to him who speaks, that we might know not only his resources but know him.

Obviously, this book is small. It is not an exhaustive treatment of the text. Rather, a few pages will be devoted to each section. The idea is to set you on the track that you might progress as you ponder these things in your heart, and to stimulate your salivary glands to taste and savor the glory and goodness of this God who is the same yesterday, today, and forever.

1. The entire account of Jehoshaphat in 2 Chron. 20:1–30 can be found at the back of this book.

1

Storm Clouds on the Horizon

A great multitude is coming against you.

Hurry, everyone into the storm cellar.” The sky grew blacker and blacker. “Dorothy, hurry up.” The whipping winds barely allowed her aunt’s words to reach her ear. “Coming, Auntie Em.” The funnel cloud moved closer and closer. “Toto, come back.” And so away went Dorothy in the film *The Wizard of Oz*, caught up in the vortex to begin her adventure over the rainbow.

In many ways, the storms of our lives resemble that classic film with the dark, ominous clouds, the whipping winds, the funnel cloud that descends to the ground making its way unstoppably and inexorably forward with us right in its path. Somewhere, way up high, even to the heavenlies, is found the rainbow of God's perfect purpose. It's there, and often the only way to see it is through the vehicle of the storm.

Clouded Vision

Oftentimes all we see is the threat, the danger—and make no mistake, it is real. Hard times are in store. As our Lord Jesus assured us of his rule over the storm, so he assured us that in this world we will face the storms of trouble (John 6:33). We are counseled by him not to worry and at the same time alerted to trouble that a day holds for us—and the measure of his grace that is sufficient for it (Matt. 6:34).

The harshness of adversity, whether it is by human hand or natural disaster, is painful, unnerving, and fearful. But in the sweeping scope of a sovereign and all-wise God there is so much more to what we encounter than meets the eye.

Pressing Problems

Just as Jesus forewarned us of the juggernaut of life, ominous and unstoppable, so Jehoshaphat received word of a mighty horde that was surging forward. And it was aimed right for him.

> After this the Moabites and Ammonites, and with them some of the Meunites, came against Jehoshaphat for battle. Some men came and told Jehoshaphat, "A great multitude

is coming against you from Edom, from beyond the sea; and, behold, they are in Hazazon-tamar" (that is, Engedi). (2 Chron. 20:1–2)

These peoples were Judah's neighboring nations. We could spend time reviewing some of the conflict, but let's just say that they had a history, which means that their approach was a severe threat. They were coming as neighbors but not neighborly. They approached as adversaries, intent on harm. This coalition of armies is characterized as a "great multitude," a vast horde. They had already advanced as far as Engedi. And they had their sights set on Jehoshaphat. No wonder those words struck terror in his heart.

It Knows Where You Live

What does the threat in your life look like? Does it have a name? Or maybe it's nebulous and nameless, but it still creates in you a panic. Are you right in the midst of it, feeling its effects, reeling under its force? Or, maybe it's something still on the horizon. Your encounter with it is inevitable. You dread it.

What exactly is so frightening about the threat, the danger, the hardship, the distress you face? What harm does it pose? Is it financial? Physical? Spiritual? Relational? Maybe the threat is not even to you directly. It's to someone you love. And for that reason, it's a threat to you as well.

Sound the Alarm

When I was in elementary school, I can well remember the air-raid drills we used to conduct. The distinctive alarm would sound and all the little boys and girls would be herded to a location or told to assume a position. Either we would be under our desks or pressed against the hallway wall. Then the all clear was given and we had to abandon the excitement to get back to work.

The point of the alarm was to sound the alert. It commanded our attention. It called for action, immediate action. No dawdling.

It works the same way when our pounding hearts or sweating palms or sleepless nights or distracted minds tell us something is up. It's lurking out there. Or, it's already in the house. These alarms that break the solace and silence of normal life command our attention and call for action.

In Action

Something needs to be done. Ignoring it won't help. I've seen that with suspected cancer. People ignore it, dreading the news. Yet the possible news itself holds them captive in the chains of fear and prevents them from doing something about it. Do you run? Do you hide? Do you inflate yourself in false bravado, insisting that you can handle it? Maybe you take the ostrich approach, burying your head in the sand of denial. After all, if you can't see it it isn't there.

What do *you* do in the face of adversity? What position do you take when you can see the whites of the eyes of an adversary?

Maybe your track record isn't so good. But God is always growing us. He is a faithful God, an ever-present help in trouble. He perseveres with us in our stubbornness, forgetfulness, weakness, pride, laziness, and all those other things that take us one step back before we take the two steps forward.

Empowerment

God's instruction to us, his equipping of us to give us voice in time of distress does not end in verse 2, where Jehoshaphat is alerted to the threat. We already know that life holds trials, troubles, and travails for us. Nobody needs to remind us of that.

In the ministry of our God to us through Jehoshaphat, God goes on in the biblical narrative. The text magnifies the threat. It's huge. It's overwhelming. It's more than we can handle. And it's right at our doorstep.

But our attention is not drawn into the bowels of the threat, to count the vast horde of warriors, to conduct inventory of their weapons, or to measure their proximity. God speaks to us by turning our attention to Jehoshaphat. What does our redirected gaze find? "Then Jehoshaphat was afraid" (v. 3). We turn up the volume and we can hear his knees knocking together. That fear sparked by the menace is a fear that knits our hearts to Jehoshaphat. Because we know what that fear is like. We can relate to the palpable sense of helplessness that induces palpitations of our heart.

God does one other thing in drawing our attention to Jehoshaphat. Not only can we relate to him in his fear, our interest is piqued. We find ourselves on the edge of our seats wondering how he will handle it. What will he do? Because it is there we find the counsel of God in our hour of need.

Taking the Reins

That's how our Lord wants to minister to us, by turning our eyes from the juggernaut to Jehoshaphat, from the threat to the threatened. He separates for us the situation from the person. In so doing, he focuses on our responsibility. How will we handle the situation? How will we handle ourselves?

That's the way God works. He wants us to guard ourselves. We are to manage ourselves in whatever circumstance he might bring into our lives.

We see this demonstrated elsewhere in the Bible. When the apostle Paul met with the Ephesian elders to give them instructions for the care of the flock, listen to what he says:

> Pay careful attention to yourselves and to all the flock, in which the Holy Spirit has made you overseers, to care for the church of God, which he obtained with his own blood. (Acts 20:28)

What order of items for attention do you notice in the apostle's admonition? The elders were to pay careful attention *first* to themselves and *then* to the flock under their care. In speaking of believers facing persecution, Paul zeroes in on personal responsibility in the circumstance: "If possible, so far as it depends on you . . . " (Rom. 12:18). Situations of threat require that we take the reigns of our lives to act and not merely to react.

Suffering in Silence

I was out for a walk in my suburban neighborhood. The day was spectacular. Spring had finally gotten a foothold. Blue sky. Greening grass. Budding trees. Warming temperatures. It was a great day to be alive. On my trek I encountered a woman I had not seen before. As we approached one another, I greeted her with a "Hi. How are you?" Her response belied our surroundings: "Hanging in there." As she hurried by I wondered what all lay behind her forlorn testimonial. Was it just a greeting or was it reflective of a distressed heart?

How many of us are just "hanging in there?" Perhaps by a mere fingernail. Trying to cope. Trying to tread water but growing more and more weary. The fabric of our lives becomes frayed and begins to unravel. We start to panic and despair. We just want to give up.

But God speaks into our distress to give us voice. He points us to someone besieged by menace. What does Jehoshaphat do? To what does our God point us as we swallow hard, our throats parched with fear that we might find utterance and even confidence that we might press on, not merely to cope but with hope?

2

Seeing beyond the Storm

Jehoshaphat was afraid and set his face to seek the L*ORD*.

We probably should not have taken off. The black clouds rolled in. Ominous peals of thunder reverberated in the distance. A light show flashed on the horizon charged with electricity. As we taxied to the runway, the first heavy drops of water fell to the tarmac, a prelude to a downpour. But the jet engine idled as we stood in the queue, waiting our turn to take off.

Though it was mid-day, the darkness suggested night had fallen. Blackness and bleakness dominated our view. Everywhere we looked it was there. We could not escape it.

The rumble of the engine inched us forward until there were no more planes in front of us. The pilot negotiated the turn onto the runway. The engine roared and the mass of metal surged forward. In a moment we were airborne, heading directly into the mouth of the storm.

As we climbed, the darkness swallowed us whole. The wind buffeted us about. But as quickly as the darkness had dominated, it gave way to brilliance as we broke through the clouds. The sun with its warmth and light greeted us on the other side. Though the clouds had obscured it, the sun was still there, communicating stability, giving its light of hope and encouragement. All was well.

The God Who Is There

Sometimes when great distress comes into our lives, it dominates us to such a degree that it's all we can see. Everywhere we turn it is there, encompassing us from all sides. It will not allow us to ignore it. And sometimes it seems the only reality.

But just as the sun remains in all its beauty, glory, and promise, so God remains. The prayer of Jehoshaphat invites us to break through the storm clouds of our distress to see that God is still there, offering hope and stability and promise. The storm is not the final word. It is not the ultimate reality. As ominous as it is, it is only for a season, irrepressibly present but irrevocably fleeting.

In the face of the foe without and the fear within, we are told that Jehoshaphat "set his face to seek the LORD."

His eyes of faith penetrated the blackness of the storm that advanced toward him. God was still there. The storm clouds had not driven him away or usurped his position as Sovereign Lord God Almighty. The brightness of his glory filled the expanse, despite appearances to the contrary.

See and Seek

Jehoshaphat not only saw that God was there, he sought this God. Three times in verses 3 and 4 we read of Jehoshaphat and the people seeking the Lord. It was Jehoshaphat's leadership that set the tone and led the way to God.

It's not as if God were playing a game. He hides while we seek. God is not being elusive, evasive, or esoteric. We are not to seek him as one hidden. We are to seek him as one revealed. He is an ever-present help in trouble. He is the God who is available, ready to be approached in time of need. That's how we seek him.

Seeking the Lord is the gracious summons of the God who wants his people to approach him. He wants us to know him, to turn to him for help in times of trouble that we might find mercy and grace to help in those times of need. Seeking him does not involve searching for him. Seeking him involves turning to him, focusing our gaze, seeing beyond the storm to behold him who reigns. The obstacle is not God, but us in our attentiveness to him.

When I was fifteen I "borrowed" my grandmother's car without her knowledge. A friend and I decided to go for a joy ride. With my judgment impaired from being under the influence, I ended up having a close personal encounter with a tree. The tree won. My grandmother's freshly inspected car was totaled. In the days before air bags, my lip hit the steering wheel and split all the way to my nose. As bad as it was, God gave me a gentle lesson. My friend and I survived. Maybe it was better that the courts did not allow me to get my driver's license until I was seventeen.

The curious thing about that crash was that there were no skid marks. It's not as though the brakes had failed. I had failed to engage them. In my panic and inexperience I had no reflex to apply the brakes.

Often in crisis, we lose our wits. The crisis consumes us and we don't think straight about what we should do. God invites us to seek him, but we don't. We forget. We neglect. It's for that reason we need to be reminded to seek him. He is there. He is available. He presents himself to be sought.

Purposed Attention

We are told that Jehoshaphat "set his face" to seek God. The idea is to give himself over. Instead of giving himself over to the storm, to be overwhelmed by it, he instead turned his gaze to God. He purposed to do so. He kept his wits about him to apply the brake to his fear instead of careening out of control in the face of menace.

In fact, Jehoshaphat not only fixed his gaze, he proclaimed a fast. Fasting is not some sort of gift we would bring to God like bringing a present with us when visiting someone in authority so that we might gain access or curry favor. Fasting was an aid to setting his face and the people's faces. Fasting is deprivation (ordinarily from food) that empties us of self, infuses us with humility and deepens a profound sense of dependency on him who provides us with our sustenance. Fasting earns us nothing. Fasting creates an atmosphere of the heart that helps us to fasten our gaze on God. It sharpens the visual acuity of our faith. It accentuates our spiritual senses, so that we are less distracted and more attracted to this God against those elements that would compete for our attention.

Trained to Turn

That is no easy task. How do we do it? How do we keep our wits in the chaos of crisis? How do we seek God at the outset instead of turning to him well into our skid as the tree approaches? Or worse yet, how do we turn to God as a first resort to the audacious challenge of the adversity instead of as a last resort when all else fails?

When the doctor taps below your knee with a rubber mallet, your leg twitches forward. You don't will it to twitch. You don't calculate a reaction. It just does it. That's a reflex. I am a seasoned tennis player. That doesn't mean I'm good, but that I've had a good amount of experience in the complexities of the sport and game conditions. My best play is when I do things reflexively. Sure I have a strategy, but my attention, strokes, footwork and the rest just happen. I have trained them over time to happen. The mechanics come without thinking.

That's the way it works in setting our face to seek God in the face of crisis. We will be more inclined to seek the Lord properly in extraordinary crisis when we are accustomed to seeking him regularly in the ordinary course of our lives. The better we know God and the more we live in personal communion with him, the more likely and natural it will be for us to turn to him when we are in distress. It's like a child in need calling "Mom!" It's reflexive. That child knows mom and reaching out in need is natural.

For us that means cultivating our prayer lives. It means living in the presence of God. Our ambition becomes to make our lives noisy with the murmur of prayer in dialog with God, praising him, thanking him, conversing with him, delighting in him.

But isn't it contradictory that setting our faces to seek God is both intentional and reflexive? The relationship between the two is nothing more than training ourselves in what we know we need to do. When we first establish any pattern or skill we need to be quite focused and deliberate about what we do. But with practice it becomes second nature. Even once learned, just like an athlete needs to make adjustments when his or her game is off, so we may need to revisit our practice of prayer.

Always There

Those storm clouds can be frightening, especially when you're flying right into them. Yet, the darkness and peril of the storm often make the light and peace of God all the more resplendent with glory, warming us, comforting us, encouraging us, giving remedy to the seasonal affective disorder that threatens to overwhelm us in those periods of peril in our lives.

These storms actually become occasions to cast ourselves upon our God. We are not to give up but to give it up, casting our cares upon him. Storms are opportunities to turn to him who is and who remains the same yesterday, today, and forever.

God invites our approach to learn of him and invokes great promise to lean upon him. He beckons us to seek him. Through the prophet Jeremiah God says to his people in peril:

> For I know the plans I have for you, declares the LORD, plans for wholeness and not for evil, to give you a future and a hope. Then you will call upon me and come and pray to me, and I will hear you. You will seek me and find me. When you seek me with all your heart, I will be found by you, declares the LORD. (Jer. 29:11–14)

God's promise to be found is a promise that he is faithful. He does not have office hours. Though all we can see sometimes are the storm clouds, he remains in place and at work, available and accessible to those whose hearts seek him.

The question is what is this God like who invites us to seek him?

3

Sharpening Our Gaze on Glory

Are you not God in heaven?

Sometimes you just want to scream. You want to go out in the middle of a field or deep in the woods or close yourself in a room and scream. It doesn't help the situation you are in, but it sure does help you. You feel better for it.

Prayer is not like that. It is not just to make you feel better by getting something off your chest or out of your system. Prayer has deeper value than unburdening ourselves. In fact, the value and power of prayer is not in itself, but in the One it addresses.

There is much written today, even in medical journals, about the cathartic and therapeutic value of prayer. It's almost like a lottery ticket. There's little chance you'll get any objective return or reward, but at least there's hope. As the advertising slogan goes, "You can't win if you don't pray" (or, is that "play"?).

Prayer, however, bears no resemblance to such therapeutic, irrational utterance. Jehoshaphat did not cry out in prayer in the face of an insurmountable behemoth that advanced against him simply to leave no option, no possibility unturned. "You never know, it might work." He did not pray to exercise a primal scream of prayer so that he would feel better.

Jehoshaphat prayed to turn to the true and living God. His cry for help was expressed not just in the direction of up, but to God Most High. He spoke to the ear of One who had invited prayer and inclines his ear to listen and to act.

A God by Any Other Name

"What a friend we have in Wilson." That might have been the title of a hymn for the character played by Tom Hanks in the movie "Castaway." Hanks had been marooned on a deserted island. A violent storm had caused the FedEx jet on which he was a passenger to crash land into the ocean. He washed ashore and was forced to survive for years on his own before being rescued.

You know how the expression goes: "There are no atheists in foxholes"? One of intriguing and improbable features of that movie was that not once did Hanks pray. What he did do, however, was find a friend in one of the FedEx boxes he opened amidst great pangs of conscience. That friend was a volleyball named "Wilson," at least that's what the label read. Hanks spends much of his time in conversation with Wilson, who was a great listener.

The problem is, Wilson could not hear, nor could "he" help. Our prayer must be directed to the one who can hear and can help. He is not a manufactured god to whom we have decided to appeal, but the Creator God who reveals himself.

The apostle Paul, in the New Testament book of Acts, visited Athens. Athens had the distinction of being the center of Greek culture, known for its philosophy, arts, and mythology. At a sort of town square Paul engaged a think tank of cutting-edge ideologues. While he toured the city he noticed altars to all sorts of gods. And, lest any god be overlooked and offended, there was a miscellaneous altar, one to an "unknown god." This etcetera altar served as the launching point for Paul in his discussion with the philosophers. He says:

> Men of Athens, I perceive that in every way you are very religious. For as I passed along and observed the objects of your worship, I found also an altar with this inscription, "To the unknown god." What therefore you worship as unknown, this I proclaim to you. (Acts 17:22–23)

Paul goes on to describe to these religious types a God who was not one of many but one. The men of Athens had made designer gods, ones that suited their own fancies, specialty gods. Paul, however, presents the God who had revealed himself and who was vastly different from the gods they had made up. He introduced them to the God who was Creator, sovereign over his creation, self-existent, self-sufficient, One to whom people were accountable, a God on whom they depended rather than the reverse. They had made gods in their own image, rather than recognizing the One in whose image they were made. Paul introduced them to the God who had introduced himself in Scripture.

All this is to say, the God we seek in prayer cannot be a made-up god. He cannot be a god of our own design or druthers. The God we seek must be the true and only God, the God who has revealed himself in his creation but especially in his Word. The Bible relays the attributes of this God and it displays his glory as Creator and Redeemer.

The Known God

Jehoshaphat approaches the God who has revealed himself. Listen to how he describes God:

> O Lord, God of our fathers, are you not God in heaven? You rule over all the kingdoms of the nations. In your hand are power and might, so that none is able to withstand you. (2 Chron. 20:6)

Jehoshaphat did not come up with these ideas himself. They are names and descriptions gleaned from God's written word over the years. Throughout the Bible, before Jehoshaphat's time and after, God is revealed. God represents himself through various names and mighty acts and surprising initiatives. We learn of him most fully in Jesus Christ, the image of the invisible God. Among the names by which God reveals himself in the pages of the Bible are: I AM, Almighty, Provider, Healer, Sovereign Lord, and Lord of hosts.

Often when God would introduce himself in times past, he would do so in a way relevant to the situation. To Abraham God introduced himself by the name "El Shaddai" (God Almighty). God wanted Abraham to know that he was able to do the impossible. He was all-powerful. That name was especially meaningful to Abraham because God had promised Abraham and Sarah they would have a child by natural means. The problem was both were old. Sarah was well beyond childbearing years, and even in her prime she had never been able to conceive. "I am El Shaddai." "I am the God who is able to back up my promises." What an encouragement to latch on to!

Name upon Name

Why does Jehoshaphat pile up names? Why does he ramble on with descriptions? Why doesn't he just say "O God" or "Sovereign Lord" and get on with it?

Sometimes when we want something from a boss we might butter him or her up a little. Is that what's going on here? Jehoshaphat is not trying to curry God's favor or influence his disposition. Nor is he just being gushingly polite. Jehoshaphat is demonstrating the pattern of many prayers of the Bible and giving us the foot on which to step out, as we would seek the God who has revealed himself.

As illustrated with Abraham, we see God speaking in times past into situations pastorally to minister to his people in times of need and to reveal his character as sufficient for that need. What descriptions of God does Jehoshaphat employ as he addresses God?

The first name is "LORD." Our English translations often use all caps to distinguish between two Hebrew names for God. An all upper case LORD refers to the name by which God revealed himself to Moses at the burning bush in Exodus 3. The bush was burning without being consumed. It was not fuel for the fire. The fire was self-existent. The name LORD is a derivative of the verb "to be." This God is self-existent. His being is eternal, inherent, and underived. Only God is like that as Creator. He does not change.

But even more specially, God revealed himself by this name to Moses on the eve of his great deliverance of his people from bondage. LORD was a name of relationship, of promise, of hope, a name peculiar to God in respect to his people. Jehoshaphat picks up on that sense in the next verse, where he recites the faithfulness of this unchanging God on behalf of his people.

In other words, Jehoshaphat was addressing God not as a stranger, not as an unknown potentate, nor an influential politician. He was addressing God by a name of great significance, importance, relevance and relationship. That name was personal, filled with familiarity.

Then Jehoshaphat goes on to address this God as God of our fathers, God in heaven, the ruler of all that is, King of kings, almighty. No king is greater than God. He raises up and brings down kings and kingdoms. No power can stand against him.

Relevant not Random

Notice that Jehoshaphat doesn't just babble on in prayer, with these descriptions of God cascading from his lips arbitrarily. He is being faced with an insurmountable, unstoppable foe. The names he uses for God assert the ability and inclination of God for help against the foe. Those names carry great meaning. They give his prayer its momentum.

God is in heaven. He is not bound by the infirmities and limitations of this world. The coalition advancing against him is indeed mighty, certainly stronger than Jehoshaphat and his forces. But these armies are not mightier than God. The enemy looked huge and daunting to Jehoshaphat but not to the God described by Jehoshaphat.

Moreover, this God rules. That means not only that God is supreme but also that the situation itself follows the direction of God's will and serves his purpose. What is that purpose? It's hard to say. But we know that God often causes deprivation to highlight our need for him. For example, we read of his dealings with his people in the wilderness:

> And he humbled you and let you hunger and fed you with manna, which you did not know, nor did your fathers know, that he might make you know that man does not live by bread alone, but man lives by every word that comes from the mouth of the LORD. (Deut. 8:3)

God wants us to grow to know him. Often, those lessons are learned in trial.

The point is that Jehoshaphat invokes the descriptions of God's revelation of himself relevant to the situation and respondent to the God who has spoken.

Praying with Your Eyes Open

What is the distress you are facing in your life? By what character qualities has God revealed himself that you can bring to bear—his power, love, mercy, grace, sovereignty, providence, wisdom, knowledge? What names of God's revelation can you invoke?

Before we pray, we want to linger. We want to reflect on the character of the God we seek. We want to rehearse those precious qualities about which he has told us. We want to see the God we are addressing. He wants us to see him.

This prayerful review of the character of God is not spinning our wheels, trying to find traction to get to the point. It is part of the point. God wants us to know him. Time spent citing and reciting the attributes of God as he has revealed himself is not primarily for God; it's for us. In so doing, we fortify our faith. We focus our faith. We fuel our faith with the octane of God's truth.

In times of crisis, we do want to rush to prayer but not rush to petition. Reflecting is to precede requesting. King Jehoshaphat nestled himself in the arms of God with each name he invoked. In those times of distress in our lives, we want to remind ourselves of the God we seek and what right of access we have. It is here that our prayer is infused with expectation.

4

Privileged Access

We will . . . cry out to you in our affliction,
and you will hear and save.

The key to prayer is the key of access. I sit to write this book at a desk of a friend who owns a business. He graciously allowed me to use a little room off his office suite that has everything I need: a desk, a door, and an electrical outlet. Since I often use his office when he is not around, my friend had a key made for me.

Early on in my use of the space, I took a mid-morning break from my writing. It was a Saturday and no one else was in the office. So I took advantage and stepped out of my room to pace and to pray. My friend's office adjoins another business. I was pacing around in front of the glass door when I noticed the owner of the other business doing something outside. He looked up and caught sight of me looking at him. The expression on his face was priceless. He wasn't used to seeing anyone in the office on Saturday, let alone a stranger. He went from being startled to becoming suspicious. What was this strange, albeit handsome, fellow doing in there? His concern had to do with right of access.

That's the way it works with prayer. If we don't have a key, we don't have right of access. On what basis do we presume to come before the presence of the Lord God Most High? It is this key that Jehoshaphat produces before he enters into petition.

God's Address

Jehoshaphat speaks next in his prayer of a sanctuary that the people have built for God. He calls it God's "house" (v. 5). He makes reference to standing before God's house to cry out to him in the face of distress.

What does it mean for God to have a house? Does God have an address? Is there somewhere we need to go in order to seek his face in prayer?

It is true that God did commission his people in the days of the kings of Israel to build a temple for him. But that did not mean that God was limited to one location or that he had office hours.

God's Dwelling

The big event, the major focus, of the book of 2 Chronicles in which we find the prayer of Jehoshaphat has to do with the temple before which Jehoshaphat stands to pray. God had appointed King Solomon, son of King David, to undertake the building of the temple. Solomon in his prayer of dedication summarizes for us what the temple is all about.

> But will God indeed dwell with man on the earth? Behold, heaven and the highest heaven cannot contain you, how much less this house that I have built! Yet have regard to the prayer of your servant and to his plea, O LORD my God, listening to the cry and to the prayer that your servant prays before you, that your eyes may be open day and night toward this house, the place where you have promised to set your name, that you may listen to the prayer that your servant offers toward this place. And listen to the pleas of your servant and of your people Israel, when they pray toward this place. And listen from heaven your dwelling place, and when you hear, forgive. (2 Chron. 6:18–21)

The temple wasn't a dwelling in which God resided, but an expression in which God dwelt among his people. It testified to God's gracious promise to dwell among his people in mercy and grace. The temple could not contain God. God fills all in all. But the temple served as a visible reminder of God's promised presence. He was present not only as the God in heaven, the Creator God, Lord of all that is. He was present as the LORD, the God their fathers, the promise-making, promise-keeping God, the one whom Jehoshaphat can call "*our* God."

The temple spoke of a special relationship initiated by God. The placement of God's physical house of stone did not impose any sense of limitation on God. Rather, it exposed the gracious personal presence of God among those on whom he had set his favor.

Expectant Prayer

Jehoshaphat stood before the temple not because he had to "go to a church building" to pray. He stood before the house of God because this God had not only promised his presence but he had promised access to that presence. He assured them he would hear.

That's the gist of Jehoshaphat's preface to petition. That is the key he pulls from his pocket, a key given him by God himself. This is what Jehoshaphat prays:

> If disaster comes upon us, the sword, judgment, or pestilence, or famine, we will stand before this house and before you—for your name is in this house—and cry out to you in our affliction, and you will hear and save. (2 Chron. 20:9)

For God's name to be "in this house" is for God's personal presence to dwell among his people. When Jehoshaphat speaks of standing before God and crying out in times of distress, he is not presuming upon God that he will "hear and save." He is taking God up on his offer expressed to Solomon for his people. God had put himself in the position of accessibility.

Seek and You Will Find

God had granted Jehoshaphat a key, not only for right of access, but affixed to the key chain of privilege and promise. After Solomon had prayed his prayer of dedication of the house of God, God issued this pledge:

> Then the LORD appeared to Solomon in the night and said to him: "I have heard your prayer and have chosen this place for myself as a house of sacrifice. When I shut up the heavens so that there is no rain, or command the locust to devour the land, or send pestilence among my people, if my people who are called by my name humble themselves, and pray and seek my face and turn from their wicked ways, then I will hear from heaven and will forgive their sin and heal their land. Now my eyes will be open and my ears attentive to the prayer that is made in this place. For now I have chosen and consecrated this house that my name may be there forever. My eyes and my heart will be there for all time. (2 Chron. 7:12–16)

As God had brought the distress for his purposes, so he had provided the promises of his presence and access to him in the midst of the distress. The temple is not a fortress, but a house of prayer. Not merely a place to go to pray, but a place where God opens himself to be sought, to be exalted and entreated.

God pledges himself to be attentive to his people. Yet access is on his terms. Seeking his face means approaching him on those terms. He wants to be sought according to his means, not only with our voice lifted up to him but also with our heart inclined to him. Requesting of God is not like turning to one of a hundred vending machines that fill the marketplace around us. He has brought his name to dwell in one place. That means we need to turn to that one place he has provided, armed with his writ of access.

The Approachable God

What is God telling us? He informs us that he extends himself as the God who is and who is approachable. He is a God on whom we can cast our cares—at his invitation, because he cares for us. God reminds you of his personal presence and accessibility in times of distress.

But he is also a God who directs in how he can be approached. His provision for access is real, but it is he who defines it. God directs our attention to that way of approach.

The temple was God's idea, his initiative. It would symbolize his presence. The temple would serve to convey the majestic transcendence of the holy God, and at the same time communicate the merciful immanence of this God who graciously purposed to dwell among those people he had taken as his very own.

More than that, God had promised admission to his presence. He promised to be there for his people, in whatever predicament they found themselves. Sometimes we face trials given us by our God for our growth and character. Other times we face troubles because of the mess we have gotten ourselves in. There are those times when we suffer under the hand of unjust persecution. In all the above and in whatever threat we may face, the God of heaven inclines his ear to us as a Father to his children.

And when God inclines himself to our distress, he offers himself not just as a listening ear, but a God who will hear and answer the pleas of his people.

Confident Prayer

Our prayer is not presumptuous. It arises from a position of privilege. It comes to us as a right of grace. Such prayer gives us audience with the living and true God because God himself has opened that access. Listen to God's understanding, compassionate, and tender invitation to those in distress who know him:

> Fear not, for I am with you; be not dismayed, for I am your God; I will strengthen you, I will help you, I will uphold you with my righteous right hand. (Isa. 41:10)

God issues his promise of presence and provision in Isaiah 41:10 from the fountain of Isaiah 41:8–9, in which he addresses the offspring of "Abraham, my friend," those whom God has "called" and "chosen." Jehoshaphat speaks in his prayer to God of "Abraham your friend" and then follows up with the precious presence of God and the promise of access and help in distress. Prayer is the conversation of grace, privilege of access to God who initiates and enters into relationship.

The Master Key

It's an amazing thought. God wants to be sought. He wants us to turn to him. So often we're used to those in power, to those with means, being hard to get to. All sorts of bureaucratic red tape. Appointments that have to be made months in advance. Not so with God. He invites us to turn to him, anytime, anywhere. And he has provided the key to enter his presence and come before him with our needs. He graciously offers that key to those on whom he has set his favor.

Listen to these words of access and invitation:

> Since then we have a great high priest who has passed through the heavens, Jesus, the Son of God, let us hold fast our confession. For we do not have a high priest who is unable to sympathize with our weaknesses, but one who in every respect has been tempted as we are, yet without sin. Let us then with confidence draw near to the throne of grace, that we may receive mercy and find grace to help in time of need. (Heb. 4:14–16)

We have a key, *the* key to his personal, powerful presence. That key is Jesus Christ. There is no other mediator between God and man. He is the true and ultimate Temple, where God dwelt among us and we behold his glory, glory of the only Son from the Father. Christ is God incarnate. In him the fullness of the Godhead dwells in bodily form. God himself has provided the means by which he can be approached to find mercy and grace to help in time of need.

In turning to God through Christ, we can have absolute and utmost confidence. Confidence that we will be heard. Confidence that we will find provision that will sustain us in our hour of need.

An Open Door

When the intruder breaks into our home and shatters our peace, when fear pours into our hearts like the rupture of a sewage tank. At those times of severe adversity when every sinew of our being is called to attention in the face of threat, we do not need to fumble around to find the right key to turn the deadbolt and rush for help. Our God presents himself as an ever-present help in trouble. We need not fear.

The key is not only ours. The door stands open. It has been opened by Christ. He *is* the door (John 10:9). When hard times press upon us and those drops of sweat bead up on our foreheads and the first wave of fear washes over us, we can rush immediately into the arms of our God. Right then, right there, right here, right now. We can rush into arms that are already open and extended to our cry, inviting us to express our deepest distress.

Here we find the irony of the temple imagery as it blossoms in Christ. A temple is a stone edifice to which people go. But Christ came to us and made *us* a temple in which he dwells by his Spirit. Our access to God is always immediate because we live in his presence and our access is continuous. We are always online.

In times of distress, God gives us recourse. He grants access to him whose resources are without limit and wisdom without fault. It is to him we express our fears. It is to this God who knows our anxious thoughts better than we do ourselves and who is able to do more than we ever could that we turn. In his plea, Jehoshaphat casts himself on this God who has promised to be found by those who seek him, and to give mercy and grace for help to those who lean upon him.

5

Prevailing Prayer

We do not know what to do, but our eyes are on you.

My favorite movie of all time is *King Kong*, the 1933 black and white original. Amazing special effects before the heyday of special effects. It is indeed a classic movie and a classic story line. "It wasn't the planes that got him; 'twas beauty that killed the beast." So opined Carl Denham, the movie director whose idea it was to venture to uncharted Skull Island in search of Kong, as the behemoth lay vanquished, having plummeted from the pinnacle of New York City's Empire State Building.

As with all great movies in that genre, the star of *King Kong* does not make his appearance until well into the film.

Anticipation mounts. Tension is created. The viewer is drawn more and more into the film and with ever-widening eyes.

In the same way, we have now come to the centerpiece of the prayer of Jehoshaphat—Jehoshaphat's prayer. The center point for us is not the behemoth; it is the petition in the face of it. Jehoshaphat cries out to God in his distress, laying before him his petition in the face of the daunting foe. What will he say? What plea will he make to the eternal, immortal, invisible, only-wise God? As a boy calls to his dad for help, what request will he make? As a pauper petitions a prince, for what resources will he appeal? We find ourselves on the edge of our seats, drawn into the drama, waiting to be instructed for the crises of our own lives.

"O our God, will you not execute judgment on them? For we are powerless against this great horde that is coming against us. We do not know what to do, but our eyes are on you" (v. 12). This prayer positions us in the hand of our God. It is here that we find voice in our distress. It leads us to find strength in weakness, courage in dependence, and confidence in trust.

Will You Not Judge Them

"Judge!"—We don't know what to make of that. What an odd way to begin a prayer! What does "judging" have to do with anything, even in Jehoshaphat's situation? How can such a request of God find a place in our prayers for the trials, troubles, and crises we face?

In glancing over some children's materials in the church in which I serve as pastor, I was surprised to see this prayer of Jehoshaphat from 2 Chronicles 20:12 among the lessons. Well, almost all of the prayer. Actually, the prayer given for the children's study and memorization was: "We are powerless against this great horde that is coming against us. We do not know what to do, but our eyes are on you."

What was missing in the petition was: "O our God, will you not execute judgment on them?" We can understand its omission. We don't know what to do with it. It doesn't seem to fit the personal, relational, financial, spiritual, emotional distress we face, at least not most of the time. Plus, it seems so caustic, so harsh, so imprecatory.

Yet call for God to execute judgment cannot be excised from the prayer. For one thing, the rest of the prayer is logically connected to this call. It flows out of a "for." More than that, the call for judgment is the actual petition. The rest of verse 12 is admission, addendums to the petition. It's like our asking a friend to open the door, because our hands are full and we're losing our grip on what we're carrying, a single request with associated reasons.

God Our Defender

Actually, the word used for "judge" here is the same word imbedded in the name Jehoshaphat. Earlier we said that Jehoshaphat means, "The Lord has judged." The "shaphat" part of his name is the same word used in his plea to the

Lord. In one sense, Jehoshaphat is bringing into play his own name as God's appointed leader of God's people.

In asking God to execute judgment, Jehoshaphat is invoking God's intervention. He is asking God to stand in the breech between him and the threat. He is calling on God to hear and to act on his behalf.

The plea cuts two ways. On the one hand, Jehoshaphat wants God to take up his cause. In his prayer of dedication of the temple we saw earlier in 2 Chronicles 6, Solomon asked God to judge by doing what was right (2 Chron. 6:23). Jehoshaphat wants God to stand between him and the enemy and uphold what was right in keeping with God's character, purpose, and promise.

When my son was eleven years old he was out playing in our neighborhood. One day I was at home doing something with my daughter in our driveway when one of the neighborhood kids came up and told me that a bunch of boys had cornered my son. The nearest and quickest means of transportation was his sister's small pink bicycle. So I jumped on the bike and peddled as fast as I could to where the boy had told me my son was. As I approached, I saw my son standing alone on a lawn with half a dozen boys threateningly spread out in front of him on the road. From a distance I shouted, "What's going on here?" The boys quickly dispersed. I got off the bike and ran to my son. Together we walked the rest of the way home.

That's what Jehoshaphat is asking of God. In the face of the threat he wants God to intervene, to protect. He wants

God not to allow the opponent to carry out its malevolent intent, but instead to uphold what is right.

On the other hand, Jehoshaphat intercedes for God to intervene because the glory and righteousness of God are at stake. Jehoshaphat and his people were called by God's name. It was not just the well-being of Jehoshaphat but the honor of God with whom he was aligned that was on the line. His request was not merely for self-preservation but for the upholding of the glory of God. He calls upon the God with whom he has relationship to act in his power, his wisdom, his promise, to uphold his cause.

That's what we pray when we ask God to execute judgment. We pray in light of our predicament and in view of God's purpose. God's intervention doesn't concern just our relief. It expects and desires the purpose of God and cries out for him to uphold what is right, as that is determined by his discretion.

It may be you are in distress because of unjust treatment. What might your prayer be? You might ask God for justice. After all, does not the Bible say elsewhere:

> If possible, so far as it depends on you, live peaceably with all. Beloved, never avenge yourselves, but leave it to the wrath of God, for it is written, "Vengeance is mine, I will repay, says the Lord." (Rom. 12:18–19)

Your distress may be prompted by something out of your control. Or, it may be your turmoil is the consequence of your own error or sin. Whatever the case, you call out for your Father in heaven to rush to your side, to undertake for you, to stand in the gap between you and the threat so that he might do what is right for your good and his glory.

We Are Powerless

How can Jehoshaphat say he is powerless? He has at his command an army of his own. Actually, his assertion of powerlessness is in respect to the foe that faces him. He is powerless against the "vast horde" advancing against him. It's like looking at a one million dollar debt and then at our one hundred dollar savings account and saying, "I'm broke." Or, facing some terminal disease for which there are no sure medications or treatments a person is constrained to acknowledge, "I'm helpless."

It's not a matter of not being able to do something. It's a matter of not being able to do enough. Our resources don't match the requirements. Our means don't measure up to the ordeal. The breadth of our shoulders is not sufficient for the burden.

In saying this, we are admitting to God that we don't have what it takes to deal with what it is we face. The adversary is too strong. The adversity too great. We state the obvious and adopt a posture of realistic humility. We take off our glasses, rose-colored with naive optimism and fitted with the distorted lenses of pride, and we humble ourselves and pray.

We Don't Know What to Do

Not only do we plead impotence, we plead ignorance. Notice that Jehoshaphat does not come with a solution in hand. He simply casts his cares upon his God in keeping with the nature of the predicament.

Doesn't that capture the panic of crisis? We are at our wit's end. We are at a loss to know what to do, where to start, even what is best.

How many times have we paced the floor, racking our minds for how best to handle a situation? Maybe it's a family crisis. Our father has left our mother. Our daughter has fallen into the insidious grip of drugs. Our powerlessness is magnified and we don't know how to go about doing what we can do.

How many times have we sat behind a table or a desk and buried our heads in our hands devoid of devices to deal with it all? We knew it would catch up with us one day. Credit cards maxed out. The well of money bone dry. The garment of façade threadbare.

Not only do we humble ourselves and pray. We seek the face of God from whom we may well have turned, on whom we may have turned our back to pursue that which he alerted was folly. That's all we have. But that's all we need.

It's remarkable the degree of powerlessness with which Jehoshaphat comes before God. He doesn't tout his own-forces and tell God he needs more. He doesn't ask God to add to his own strength. He doesn't even bring suggestion to God how to go about intervening.

Such an abject plea lays the entirety of the situation before God. Not only do we look to God in our weakness, we seek him in our strength. Not only do we cry out to our God in our inability, we cry out in our ability. We want his strength, his wisdom. He alone knows what is right for his good and perfect purposes.

Our Eyes Are On You

When I'm at the kitchen counter, I almost always have company—Oscar. Oscar is my miniature black and tan dachshund. And he's full of expectation. He sits there in silence, but I can feel his presence. I can sense his doleful eyes boring into me. I look down determined that I won't give him any of my human food. After all, Oscar has a perfectly good dish of dog food a few feet away. But I always capitulate, and surrender some of my own food.

God has purposed to be merciful, not to treat us as our sins deserve. He has provided a means to come before him, even shame-faced in our folly, even when we are reaping what we have sown; in his grace, he opens his hand to provide what we neither deserve nor can claim as a right.

This is the God Jehoshaphat sees when he says that his eyes are upon God. The God he beholds reigns over all and is mighty to save, a bulwark for those whose trust is in him. He is the LORD, the God of their fathers, and their God. He is the omnipotent God who invites his people to prevail upon him and to avail themselves of his wisdom, grace, and power.

The God to whom we turn our eyes in times of crisis must be the God who has revealed himself in his Word. We want to fill our gaze with the full spectrum of God's glory. We turn to God not just for a hand out, but with hands up, raised in praise and awe. He is the God who works all things for the good of those who love him and belong to him, and he alone is the determiner of that good. He will not give stones for bread. The gold of his blessing is never pyrite and the calories of his provision are never empty. He is the God whose ways are inscrutable to us but whose wisdom is perfect and plans are without flaw. The clearer we see God, the greater will be our peace, our resolve, our stability. In this way, we can turn to God with expectation.

And just as Oscar waits in expectation, so we lift our eyes to this God of glory and promise and keep our gaze riveted upon him. In Christ, we have reason to expect. As we wait upon the Lord, we will find vigor and valor to meet the distress.

Learning to Lean, Leaning to Learn

In *King Kong*, it was not the planes of might or the plans of men that got him; it was beauty that felled the beast. The mammoth gorilla simply refused to let go of his first love that filled his heart and fueled his ambition.

Jehoshaphat's prayer reflects a heart that refused to turn elsewhere and would instead trust in his faithful Lord, desiring him to do what was right. He would jettison his own resources, ingenuity, and ambitions and would lean upon the God of promise.

We often play the role of Kong. And it may well be that the distress has come into our lives because God wants us to have no mistress, no competitor for allegiance to him. He wants our whole heart, to love him with all our heart and mind and soul and strength. He wants our eyes on him. Sometimes he brings us to the end of ourselves to learn of him who is boundless in love, power, and wisdom.

With Kong, we may think the strength of our brains or brawn or beauty or whatever else we suppose gives us leverage will rule the day. We climb the pinnacle of what the world has to offer, following the instinct of our misguided sensibilities. But instead God brings us to rue the day we assumed such a posture, as that folly of pride becomes our downfall. All the while his ear is attentive to our cry, as the voice of a son to his father. He invites us to listen to him, to lean on him, and to learn his sufficiency for our need.

6

Sand Bags of Promise

Thus says the L*ORD* *to you.*

The ominous clouds of the storms of our lives often obscure our view of the glory of God who abides in the heavens, faithful and unchanging. But those same clouds can close in upon us to such a degree that they dominate our attention and distract us from those who stand with us.

A Wider Swath

Our eyes have been fixed on Jehoshaphat. Our ear has been attentive to his prayer. Now the camera shifts and pans the crowd: "Meanwhile all Judah stood before the

LORD, with their little ones, their wives, and their children" (2 Chron. 20:13).

Not only do we feel the sense of desperation, we are also reminded of the stakes. When a husband finds himself ensnared in the tightening coils of pornography, it is not only he who is affected. His wife and children may well become casualties of his folly. When a woman is overwhelmed with the news of her ovarian cancer, her husband and children and coworkers and friends are caught up in the wake.

Take a look at the situations of distress of your life. Who would suffer along with you in the crisis that has opened its mouth to swallow you up? Whom does your sin or addiction to which you have given yourself place in harm's way? Who joins you to sleep in the bed you have made because of your indiscretions? The storms of our lives often cut a path that impacts others as well.

So often in harm's way we are not alone. The camera pans back from our own distress and we see the faces of those we love. And so our prayer encompasses not only ourselves but these ones as well. As they have seen our taking leave of self and turning to God, they, too, stand with a sense of expectation. Along with us they wait on the Lord. They are in the same boat. They have no power to face the foe. They do not know what to do. But their eyes are on God.

The Posture of Prayer

Jehoshaphat has just cried out to the Lord for his intervention, acknowledging his own impotence and ignorance.

The plea has gone up to God. He is the God who is able to do all things, the God who has promised to incline his ear to the pleas of his people. He will hear and he will act. The send button on the prayer has been pressed. Now the wait. How will the Lord respond? When will he respond?

These questions are answered from the posture of prayer. We're not talking about standing to pray or kneeling to pray. The posture of prayer speaks to the position of the heart as ones needy and dependent, but expectant at the same time.

Great Expectations

Playing the lottery is more than a gamble; it is grasping for unlikely gain. When you hear that you have a greater chance of being hit by lightning than winning the lottery, only starry-eyed optimism fuels hope. But the hope of answered prayer that generates confidence and great expectation is realized every time. God does and will answer prayer that proceeds from the heart that knows and seeks him.

Because God does commit himself to answer prayer, when we pray we watch in expectation for his response. The psalmist says:

> Give ear to my words, O LORD;
>   consider my groaning.
> Give attention to the sound of my cry,
>   my King and my God,
>   for to you do I pray.

O LORD, in the morning you hear my voice;
in the morning I direct my prayer to you and watch.
(Ps. 5:1–3[1])

Prayer puts us on the alert. God has pledged himself to attend to the prayers of his people. So we watch. We wait with expectation. Not that we wait in silence. We continue to keep current our distress in the ear of our God as long as that distress is current in our lives. Jesus' statement: "Will not God give justice to his elect, who cry out to him day and night?" concludes his parable as he began: "And he told them a parable to the effect that they always ought to pray and not lose heart" (Luke 18:1, 7).

To Refer Is to Defer

Not only do we wait upon the Lord, we wait with the same posture in which we approached the Lord. The same humbling of self that brought us to prayer and carried our prayer is the humility of submission and deference in which we wait.

When we submit our requests to God in prayer, we submit our wills as well. "Your will be done, on earth as it is in heaven," is assumed in prayer that knows and seeks God. That posture of submission refers not only to *how* God answers, but *when*. God, in his infinite wisdom, may answer our prayer with a "yes," "no," "not now," "not in the way you think best."

1. Alternate reading, footnoted in ESV text.

Jehoshaphat had cast his cares upon the Lord. He had humbled himself before God. He had left his prayer open-ended, deferring to God's wisdom and ways.

God Speaks

Although God does answer prayer in his way and in his time, God does not make Jehoshaphat wait long. The next verse tells us that the Spirit of the Lord came upon one of the priests whose name was Jahaziel. He brings the Word of God, the answer to prayer, not only to the king but to the whole assembly.

To say, "the Spirit of the LORD came upon" (2 Chron. 20:14) is the classic biblical presentation of a person being endowed by God for prophetic utterance.

Jahaziel, under the superintendence of the Holy Spirit, speaks the inspired Word of God. He begins, "Listen, all Judah and inhabitants of Jerusalem and King Jehoshaphat: Thus says the LORD to you, 'Do not be afraid and do not be dismayed at this great horde, for the battle is not yours but God's'" (v. 15).

What amazing words of compassion, comfort, and encouragement! God has given ear to your plea, says the prophet. Now give ear to God. That's what we want. In the face and the fear of the storm we desperately want to hear from God. We want words of comfort, assurance of care, encouragement of hope. What is God's answer to us? Where is God's Spirit-anointed prophet to speak to us in our distress?

Inspired of God

God tells us that he has spoken in his Word, the Bible. "All Scripture is breathed out by God" (2 Tim. 3:16). The Bible is the very word of the living God. In the Bible it is the Holy Spirit who ministers the Word of God through his human agents. Though the words spoken are those of the person writing, they are ultimately the words of God himself. Thus the "thus says the LORD" (2 Chron. 20:15).

As with the prophets of old, those mouthpieces of God by whom he ministered to his people and provided them with firm footing and sure direction, so the Bible is inspired of the Spirit of God through human instruments. God assures us that "no prophecy was ever produced by the will of man, but men spoke from God as they were carried along by the Holy Spirit" (2 Peter 1:21).

Prophecy does not always or even usually refer to predictions. Typically, we think of prophecy as foretelling, such as Micah predicting where the Christ would be born seven hundred years prior to the event (cf. Micah 5:2 with Matt. 2:1–6). But ordinarily, prophecy has to do with divine utterance. Prophets are the mouthpieces of God. God speaks with truth and authority and relevance into the need of the moment. Prophecy is not produced by dictation, but by the mysterious working of God's Spirit in human instruments through their wills, experiences, and personalities to pen just what he wants expressed.

Sufficient for Our Need

"But I don't want to hear what God has spoken; I want him to speak now. I want him to speak to my life, my storm, to minister to my need." We don't want a canned response. We want a word from God that is personal, timely, and relevant.

God's Word is not archaic. It is living and active. Truth does not go out of style. God's Word is truth. The God of Jehoshaphat's day is the same God in our day. The character and the characteristics of God we find revealed in that day remain constant in this day.

In speaking of his written Word, God says that by it we are equipped with his wisdom to deal with whatever we face in this life.

> All Scripture is breathed out by God and profitable for teaching, for reproof, for correction, and for training in righteousness, that the man of God may be competent, equipped for every good work. (2 Tim. 3:16–17)

Because it is the very Word of God himself, abiding truth of an unchanging God, it will bring nourishment and refreshment for our need.

God has provided the wisdom of his Word and the power of the Spirit who inspired it to handle whatever he brings us to face. The Spirit who brings us the Bible, the Word of God, is the same One who assures us of its sufficiency. We don't need fresh revelation. Though the Word is ripe with time, it is never crusty with age. Its truth is fixed but its relevance is ever flowing, fresh and refreshing, applicable to our situation.

God's Word is a storehouse of promises. The apostle Peter, who has affirmed the divine character of the Bible by the operation of the Holy Spirit, affirms the sufficiency of God's provision for whatever life may hold:

> May grace and peace be multiplied to you in the knowledge of God and of Jesus our Lord. His divine power has granted to us all things that pertain to life and godliness, through the knowledge of him who called us to his own glory and excellence, by which he has granted to us his precious and very great promises. (2 Peter 1:2–4)

Sandbags of Promise

Just as Jahaziel bolstered the confidence and courage of Jehoshaphat and the people with the words, "Thus says the Lord," so we find sandbags of God's truth and promise stored for us in the warehouse of his Word.

And God's promises never come to us apart from his presence. As his Word is living and active so is he. The prophet Isaiah brings us the encouragement to wait on the Lord in the knowledge of his glory and in admission of our frailty:

> Have you not known? Have you not heard? The Lord is the everlasting God, the Creator of the ends of the earth. He does not faint or grow weary; his understanding is unsearchable. He gives power to the faint, and to him who

> has no might he increases strength. Even youths shall faint and be weary, and young men shall fall exhausted; but they who wait for the LORD shall renew their strength; they shall mount up with wings like eagles; they shall run and not be weary; they shall walk and not faint. (Isa. 40:28–31)

As we saw earlier, this same prophet, under the inspiration of the Holy Spirit, assures us as ones belonging to God:

> Fear not, for I am with you; be not dismayed, for I am your God; I will strengthen you, I will help you, I will uphold you with my righteous right hand. (Isa. 41:10)

"Will you not execute judgment?" we pray for God to intervene. "I will uphold you with my righteous right hand," he assures us of his abiding presence and abounding provision. The first sandbag of promise gleaned from his Word is put in place as we prepare for the storm's onslaught.

In times of trouble, battered by the winds of despair, knocked down by the waves of fear, we want to fortify our position with the sandbags of God's promise. What does God tell us about himself that is an anchor to our soul? What truths does God give us to which we can lay hold and buttress ourselves against the onslaught?

And so it is with the same ears that the words of Jahaziel minister to us when he gives founded and focused encouragement: "Do not be afraid and do not be dismayed at this great horde, for the battle is not yours but God's" (2 Chron. 20:15).

7

Standing Firm

Stand firm and see.

"Everything will be okay." How many times have those words of comfort been extended to someone in distress? As the mother anxiously waits for word on her son who is in emergency surgery, a well-meaning friend draws to her side: "Everything will be okay." The husband paces the floor wondering where his wife is. She should have been home three hours ago. She doesn't answer her cell phone. In a reversal of roles, his six-year-old son approaches his father and looking up says, "Everything will be okay, daddy." With pink slip in hand, your heart in your throat, your stomach in knots and a mortgage to pay, you try to convince yourself, "Everything will be okay."

But everything is not always okay, is it? Those words, with all their good intentions, fall as litter to the ground. Empty. Offering hope without substance. Expressing more a wish than extending a bulwark.

Terms of Encouragement

"Do not be afraid and do not be dismayed" (v. 17). So speaks the prophet of God in response to Jehoshaphat's prayer.

That's just what Jehoshaphat and the people needed to hear. In the face of daunting opposition and great threat, they needed peace to replace their panic. They needed to stop the hemorrhaging of their confidence before it all drains out of them and they find themselves as lifeless as those depleted of blood, listless for the challenge.

"Do not be afraid and do not be dismayed at this great horde." That's easier said than done. How can they not be gripped in fear? How can they not be dispirited in the face of something far beyond their capacity to handle?

A Firm Foundation

But the prophet does not stop with words of well-wishing. He plugs them into a power source. He grounds his words with that which gives them substance. It is more than an "everything will be okay." It is an "everything will be okay *because* . . . "

When we are in crisis we strain to hear the "because." We want to know why the doctor thinks the cancer will not be terminal. We press the police for why they think our child will be found. Many times we grasp for even the slightest of branches of hope to climb out of the pit of our despair.

The "because" the prophet holds out, though, is not a twig. It is a redwood. "Do not be afraid and do not be dismayed at this great horde, for the battle is not yours but God's" (v. 15). If we can have confidence and courage in knowing that the operation is not in our hands but in a surgeon who is the best in the business, how much more can we find confidence and courage in knowing that our circumstance is in the hands of him who created all that is and for whom nothing is impossible?

Wisdom and Power

I had just purchased a chainsaw, the first one I ever owned. My testosterone was surging. Eager to try out my new acquisition, I ventured out to my yard looking for victims. A couple small branches proved no match. Then I spotted a worthy opponent.

Leafy branches had been impeding my path on the slope of my yard for mowing the lawn. In inspecting how I might best trim them back I noticed that all of them extended from one limb. The limb was connected to a large maple tree and measured about thirty feet long. All I had to do was lop it off at the trunk of the tree and I could resolve my mowing obstruction in one fell swoop.

My twenty-foot ladder was too short so I borrowed my neighbor's thirty-foot ladder. I lofted it against the trunk of the tree, started my chainsaw, and climbed the siege work. The blade met no resistance as it made its way into the branch. The next thing I knew the branch was on the ground, but it had taken with it my brand new chainsaw. As I cut into the branch it snapped off suddenly, recoiled, and knocked the chainsaw right out of my hand, just missing me.

Later I talked with a friend who does tree work for a living. He told me he knew a guy who had been killed in doing just what I had done. He also explained to me the physics involved and the proper way to cut a long branch.

The moral of the story? I had the power but not the wisdom. I had the ability but not the wherewithal to wield it.

But with God both power and wisdom are resident. The "because" of the prophet's words of encouragement rested on the God who had everything necessary to win the day. For the battle to be God's was not only a statement reflecting God's care of those who bore his name. It was a statement that grounded the urging not to be afraid and not to be dismayed in the face of a fearsome foe. The words were not empty but emphatic with substance.

Refuge and Strength

God loves to give us pictures. The Bible is filled with metaphors and rich speech in which God communicates to us in vivid and meaningful ways. In Psalm 46 God communicates what he has here with Jehoshaphat, but with the impact of metaphor that draws us in to find comfort and courage. There the psalmist draws the conclusion:

> Therefore we will not fear though the earth gives way, though the mountains be moved into the heart of the sea. (Ps. 46:2)

The "therefore" emanates from the picture given of God in Psalm 46:1: "God is our refuge and strength, a very present help in trouble."

Why need we not fear? *Because* God is a refuge and strength. More than that, God is *our* refuge and strength. He is our protection in distress. He is our power in weakness. Though what we consider unmovable and unshakable lets us down, though the unexpected assails us, though the foundations of our world shake and even crumble beneath our feet, God remains. He is unshakable, unassailable, inviolable.

With Jehoshaphat we are called not to fret or fear *because* God will undertake for us who are his. The psalmist turns it around to first establish God as our firm foundation and *therefore* we need not fear. Either way we approach it, *because* or *therefore,* the foundation is the same. God is the spring of our composure, the supply of our courage.

Be Still

God is our refuge and strength; therefore we need not fear. But we do fear. We tremble before the horde that is too much for us. The psalmist in Psalm 46 issues a call to action in verse 10, telling us of first order, "to be still and know he is God."

The prophet with Jehoshaphat calls him and the people to a similar position: "Stand firm, hold your position." With that comes the expectation, "you will see the salvation of the LORD on your behalf" (2 Chron. 20:17).

There's a difference between knowing something and availing yourself of it. We can know seatbelts save lives, but strapping ourselves in is a different matter. Not only do we need to hear and know the sufficiency of our God, we need to position ourselves right there. We need to seek cover in him who is our refuge and strength. We need to align ourselves behind him whose battle it is, by virtue of his assurance.

Take a Stand

"Stand firm," the prophet brings the word of the Lord. In the face of distress and crises of our lives, those words come to us from the lips of the living and true God. Stand firm.

Current wisdom says that when an earthquake strikes, a person is to take refuge under a lintel, because, though the rest of the house collapses, that will remain intact. Our God tells us in those tremors and those seven-point-fives of our lives that we are to take our stand where we can be safe and where we find strength—with him, in the shadow of the Almighty, behind the skirts of the Lord of hosts.

There will be ample room. And he is able whatever the Richter Scale may register.

What that means is that, not only do we need to see the security of our God, not only do we need to hear his gracious invitation to find refuge in him, such a summons calls us to take stock of where we stand at the moment.

That begs the question for each of us, on what do we rest when crisis strikes or threat stalks? Where do we take our stand? Do we trust in God or the currency on which the motto is printed? Do we look to governments or him from whom all authority is given? Do we ultimately lean on physicians or him who formed us wonderfully in our mother's womb and is the Great Physician? Is our trust in the means of the police officers searching for our lost child or in him who is everywhere and from whom nothing is hidden? God may use these means, but on what do we ultimately rest?

We find that to position ourselves is often to reposition ourselves, to move from where we have been standing, to relocate from where we had sought refuge and strength. In our own wisdom, we seek safety and solace under the spreading tree from the lightning striking around us. It makes sense, but has dire consequences.

To position ourselves is to stand firm and immovable, believing our God and believing in his provision for our need. We stand with conviction. To reposition ourselves is to move from panic to peace, to forsake discouragement to find cheer and courage at the voice of our God.

Strength for Today

As with Jehoshaphat, God first comforts us. Then he confronts the adversary. Two points of attack: the fear within and the foe without. God covers both bases as he ministers to us in our distress.

As the prophet Jahaziel said it once in our text, so he repeats it: "Do not be afraid and do not be dismayed" (vv. 15, 17). Like slices of bread that bracket the contents, so God's tender and timely words of comfort hold the meat of his presence and promise. And he invites us to eat and find sustenance, nourishment, and delight in the provision of his mercies. And, just as food provides energy for action, so our standing firm in faith leads to our stepping out in faith.

8

Stepping Out

Go out against them, and the L*ORD* *will be with you.*

I could not get back in. Although only in my early teens I was a fairly strong swimmer. But the surf that day was too rough and the waves relentless. As soon as I dove in to one wall of water to avoid it crashing upon me, another took its place, drawing me further out to sea. I could feel my arms tiring. The summer crowd on the beach was oblivious to my plight, not knowing that within minutes I could lose my battle with the storm-tossed surf.

I couldn't give up, but it dawned on me that was exactly what I needed to do. My weary body in full cooperation, I became a piece of driftwood bobbing on the water's surface, being tossed about at the whim of the ocean's churning. Soon the waves became my ally instead of my enemy. Closer and closer they carried me to the safety of shore. I stretched out my leg. My foot grazed the ocean floor. With newfound energy gained from being actively passive, I reached down my other leg and started trudging to the beach and to a memory that has stayed with me to this day.

Stand and Step

You might hear that story and say, "What a perfect illustration of Jehoshaphat's prayer!" One of those "let go and let God" moments. It is true, we are to stand, to rest, to trust, to wait, but that's only half the story. Our God does want us to cast ourselves upon him. He wants us to know his sufficiency. He wants us to know that our enemy is too strong for us. But there's more.

God also wants us to act. As Peter puts it, he wants us "to commit ourselves to our faithful Creator *and* continue to do good." Trust *and* obey. That's the tandem, the marching steps, for facing the storms of life that threaten to undo us. We walk in the obedience of submission. We act. Christ is our strength, but it is "I" who is given the encouragement to do all things through him who gives that strength.

Even as we wait on the Lord, it is for refreshment, renewal, and reinvigoration so that we can run and not grow weary, walk and not faint.

Pray and Do

After the Lord's call to Jehoshaphat to "stand firm," he follows up with a call to "go out" (v. 17). Jehoshaphat is to ready himself for battle and to engage the foe.

Prayer is not a substitute for action. Nor does it preclude action. In many ways, prayer itself is action. But it also sets the stage for what God enables us to do in his power and wisdom to deal with the crisis that confronts us. We step out in the resources and opportunities our God gives us in answer to our prayers.

The Old Testament book of Nehemiah deals with a period of history in the life of God's people after the time of Jehoshaphat. God's people still faced daunting challenges and enemy opposition. The book is filled with prayer, from the moving prayer of contrition and petition of chapter one (Neh. 1:5–10), to the "popcorn" prayer of chapter two (Neh. 2:4) as Nehemiah speaks up before the king, to the extraordinary covenant chronicle prayer that occupies the whole of chapter nine.

Yet the book of Nehemiah is filled with activity as well. Prayer launches action. Prayer is the glove in which the hand of action is fitted. In Nehemiah 4 the enemy looms large. We find prayer by Nehemiah in that chapter (4:4–5) as he beseeches God to intervene against the foe. But in chapter 4 we also find the other shoe to prayer: "And we prayed to our God and set a guard as a protection against them day and night" (4:9). Pray and do. Commit the situation to God; commit ourselves to action for God.

We find the same two-pronged approach in the New Testament. In Matthew 6:11 the Lord Jesus instructs us in his model prayer to request of the Father our daily bread. In his second letter to the Thessalonians, the apostle Paul reminds them that if they refuse to work, then they shall not eat (2 Thess. 3:10). We are to pray for our daily bread and step out in the means of God's appointment to work for that bread. Pray and do, as the Lord enables, to the glory of his name.

Promise of God's Presence

"I am weak, but thou art mighty. Hold me with thy powerful hand." A sobering thought, an encouraging truth by the hymn writer.

All our lives we face things that frighten us. Probably all of us have some memory as children of something we were scared to death to do. But we gained our resolve from our mother or father who was by our side or within sight.

When God calls Jehoshaphat to "go out against them," he attaches the promise: "and the LORD will be with you." Not only does God's presence give us *comfort* in the face of our fear, it gives us *courage* to face the adversity. He is a faithful and powerful God who pledges to be with his children to minister to us in our need and to enable us to deal with whatever confronts us.

God's promised presence invites peace to guard our hearts and courage to guide our steps. What that means is that whatever confronts us in life, no matter how big or strong, we want to remind ourselves that God is not only Sovereign Lord; he is the Lord who provides. He knows the need. He knows our insufficiency. He knows his purpose. He is with us to cheer and to guide, to grant us strength for today and bright hope for tomorrow.

In other words, whatever God calls us to deal with he grants solace and strength by his personal presence to handle. The words of 1 Corinthians 10:13 give us hope not merely to weather the storm but to press on in it.

> No temptation has overtaken you that is not common to man. God is faithful, and he will not let you be tempted beyond your ability, but with the temptation he will also provide the way of escape, that you may be able to endure it. (1 Cor. 10:13[1])

The linchpin of that verse is the faithful God, who is able to do all things. The promise is not that the trial will go away, but that God is with us to handle it in a way that honors him.

Whose Battle?

If I tell my wife that I am going to do something, that means that that something is my responsibility and not hers. I would not expect her to do it. She would expect me to do it.

1. The words translated "temptation" can also be translated as "trial."

In 2 Chronicles 20:15 God said through the prophet, "The battle is not yours but God's." In verse 17 he says, "You will not need to fight this battle." Jehoshaphat and his army are to stand and see, to rest and watch.

Now God tells them to go out against the foe, to engage the foe. First, he tells them they do not need to fight the battle. Now he tells them to fight the battle. Which is it? Whose responsibility is it?

The answer is ours. Actually, the responsibility lies in both courts. But the answer to the question for our purposes is ours, because we are able to carry out only our responsibility, not God's. The fact that God rules establishes our responsibility and does not compete with it.

We see this dynamic in both Old and New Testaments, in which God's rule is primary, and establishes our role.

> O LORD, you will ordain peace for us; you have done for us all our works. (Isa. 26:12) . . . work out your own salvation with fear and trembling, for it is God who works in you, both to will and to work for his good pleasure. (Phil. 2:12–13)

The Lord's call to fight is not contradictory but complementary to the battle being the Lord's. We work for his cause. We walk in his strength. We wait on his provision.

The Tomorrow Principle

Just what can we do? When we are faced with cancer? With bankruptcy? With overwhelming loss and grief? With profound helplessness? With pain or panic that racks our soul?

We can avail ourselves of God's provision. See the oncologists. Get a second opinion. Restructure debt. Seek out a compassionate friend. All with our God who is Lord of means as well as ends.

Jehoshaphat was told to go out against the foe. Today that meant preparing the troops. Tomorrow that meant engaging the opponent.

Our Lord Jesus in the Sermon on the Mount lays out for us a helpful distinction. He divides between today and tomorrow.

> Therefore do not be anxious about tomorrow, for tomorrow will be anxious for itself. Sufficient for the day is its own trouble. (Matt. 6:34)

Today is something we can do something about. Tomorrow deals with what is not yet and may not even be. God has given us strength for the day. He dispenses his manna sufficient for the day. Though he is already there, he has not yet brought us to tomorrow. So we *consecrate* the day at hand to him, serving him with our very best, with the strength he provides. And we *commit* the day(s) ahead to him, trusting him for his care and provision when that time comes. We may plan for tomorrow, but it's always in pencil, deferring to God's will, submitting to his purpose (see James 4:13–15). One day at a time, one foot in front of the other.

Stepping Out—in Faith

Part of "today" for Jehoshaphat was the immediate expression of trust. On the heels of the prophet's word, "Tomorrow go out against them, and the Lord will be with you" follows the response of faith.

> Then Jehoshaphat bowed his head with his face to the ground, and all Judah and the inhabitants of Jerusalem fell down before the LORD, worshiping the LORD. (2 Chron. 20:18)

Jehoshaphat did not protest. He prostrated himself before the Lord who had spoken into his distress. Worship reflected an expression of courage and confidence gained from God's promised presence.

When God calls us to deal with the distress in our lives, when he doesn't just remove it from us but calls us to deal with it, what do we do? Do we worship, bowing before God who does all things well? Or, do we rebel, complain, contest, and maybe even bring God under our judgment, calling him to task?

Faith that knows and seeks God will rest in him. Worship and delight will be reasonable and necessary responses. Our fear does not rule the day. Our weakness does not determine our decisions. Worship brings God to the fore. It recognizes him as the one on the throne. And it seeks to serve him as God and not as gimmick in the very predicament in which we find ourselves.

As Far As It Concerns You

Inadequacy does not lead to inactivity. It leads to a position of dependent responsibility, to a posture of expectant mobility as we step out, fight the fight, run the race with our eyes fixed on our Lord.

Because the battle is the Lord's, it does not mean we are relegated to being mere spectators. We fight in his strength with his strategy. We worship our Lord in response to the precious promises of his presence and provision. And we step out to confront the foe as an act of worship in seeking first his kingdom and his glory.

9

Courage of Faith

Believe . . . and you will be established.

Emboldened by the Word of God and the promise of his presence, Jehoshaphat stands as leader before the people, ready to act. God has said, "go out" (v. 17). Early on the next day, the tomorrow of God's bidding, they "went out" (v. 20).

Jehoshaphat addresses the people of God:

> Hear me, Judah and inhabitants of Jerusalem! Believe in the LORD your God, and you will be established; believe his prophets, and you will succeed. (2 Chron. 20:20)

They will march to face the foe, stepping out on the foot of faith. Trust. Act. Expect. Obey. All are streams flowing out of the fountain of faith.

Faith is adrenaline that will compel us and embolden us to deal with the adversaries and the adversities we face in our lives. But how do we find courage in faith? The little boy might have faith he can handle the bully, but does that mean he really can? Faith and reality do not always mesh.

Founded Faith

Faith is not self-confidence; at least the faith on which Jehoshaphat leads his troops is not self-confidence. In fact, the faith exhibited by Jehoshaphat is the very antithesis of confidence in himself and his own abilities and resources. The king has expressly divested himself of such things. He has decried his own ability: "we are powerless against this great horde." He has denounced his own ingenuity: "we do not know what to do" (v. 12).

The athlete who faces insurmountable odds is called to have faith in himself. The child getting poor grades is told to believe in herself. Self-help gurus urge us to reach deep into our inner beings to find the resolve that gives us courage in handling the predicaments of life. Like the little engine that could, we are to chant in self-motivation, "I think I can. I think I can." Propelled by the winds of positive thinking we will scale whatever mountain we face.

God has a different plan. The faith he envisions and communicates to us is not a faith that scurries into the sheds of our inner beings to find the tools necessary for the job. The faith God calls us to is a faith that reaches out of ourselves.

Of course, the question then is, to what does faith reach out? We've already seen the only sure ground of faith—the living and true God and the illumination of his living and true Word.

Faith does not just believe as though believing had value in and of itself. Faith trusts, seeks, rests and relies on God. As *believers,* we hold fast to our God, leaning upon him when we deal with the insurmountable, the insoluble and the insufferable. Faith is the opposite of self-confidence. It is God-confidence.

Focused Faith

The confidence that compels Jehoshaphat is a confidence that finds its footing on the Lord their God, and its bearings from the Word of God brought through his prophets. Faith rests on and responds to a reality, not a wish. It is a spiritual capacity that sees and acts on the God who is there and the God who has spoken.

Perhaps no better expression of the angst of life has been captured than by the Norwegian artist Edvard Munch (1863–1944). His most famous work, *The Scream,* depicts a freeze frame of life that assaults the viewer with uncontrolled volatility. The long, multi-directional, wavy lines convey a world in disorder, disarray, and turmoil. The red hues of the sky speak not to the beauty of the setting sun, but to the panic induced by a tumultuous world that tyrannizes us. The haunting figure to which the eye is drawn can do nothing but cover his ears and scream.

But the scream is silent. Is there anyone to hear? Is there anyone to help?

The figure in *The Scream* is simply responding to what he sees. And what he sees is life assaulting him. He cannot control things. They are more than he can manage. He cannot make sense of things.

I can think of no better representation of the Old Testament book of Ecclesiastes than Munch's *The Scream.* When we look at life "under the sun," the refrain of the book, we are driven to conclude that all is but a vapor. "Vanity of vanities! All is vanity." Empty, pointless, meaningless, fleeting, oppressive, unfair. As much as we try to dig ourselves out of a hole, the walls collapse and we are left to dig and dig still more. Along with Munch's open-mouthed, ear-covered, isolated, haunting figure, we look at life that is hostile, oppressive, and relentless, and the only voice we can muster is a scream.

Fearful Faith

Faith, however, lends us a vastly different view on life. Faith sees those things in life that are unfair. Faith sees the destructive, overwhelming, unstoppable forces in life that assail us. But faith also sees where the writer of Ecclesiastes leads us. We see beyond that which is "under the sun." We look beyond the created order (i.e., under the sun) to see the Creator, to behold the God who is and who reigns.

The writer of Ecclesiastes lays out for us the bottom line.

> The end of the matter; all has been heard. Fear God and keep his commandments, for this is the whole duty of man. (Eccles. 12:13)

To fear God is not to be afraid of God, but to give him the glory and the place that belong to him. In fearing God we adopt the posture of the creature and we accept the limitations and responsibilities that go along with it. We trust to obey.

Faith finds courage because it knows and trusts God. Faith that fears God finds meaning amidst the confusion of life, purpose amidst the confounding of life, and value amidst the seeming pointlessness of life.

In other words, we head out to face the foe not fearing it or them, but fearing God. We face the foe confident of God's power, content in God's purpose. The courage of our faith is not empty bravado. Our courage is the necessary overflow of a faith that flows from the fountain of his Word and Spirit.

Come What May

But what if I go out and am defeated? What if I pray and go out to meet the crisis that confronts me and I buckle and fall? What if God does not intervene?

There are examples of that in Scripture. The most glaring is the Lord Jesus Christ. He cried out to the Father to spare him the crisis of the cross. "Father, take this cup from me. Yet not my will but your will be done." God did not spare his own Son. Yet it all unfolded according to the plan of God. It all served the purpose of God.

The outcome rests with God. Our job is to trust and obey. We are not ones to shrink back. We are not ones to shirk our responsibility. We are to be ones who venture out in the courage of faith.

Forged Faith

The three young men had been called to account. The mighty king had ordered every subject of his vast empire to bow down before the god he had made. "Whoever does not fall down and worship shall immediately be cast into the fiery furnace" (Dan. 3:6). Daniel's trio of friends refused. They would not desert the true God who made them in order to worship a god made by man. It was a matter of allegiance, of obedience.

Nebuchadnezzar was enraged. Who were these pipsqueaks to defy him? The king interrogated the young men to find out if their insubordination was true. He gave them one more chance: worship the statue or face the flames. Then the king drew the line in the sand: "Who is the god who will deliver you out of my hands?"

The three young men, Shadrach, Meshach, and Abednego, answered:

> O Nebuchadnezzar, we have no need to answer you in this matter. If this be so, our God whom we serve is able to deliver us from the burning fiery furnace, and he will deliver us

> out of your hand, O king. But if not, be it known to you, O king, that we will not serve your gods or worship the golden image that you have set up. (Dan. 3:16–18)

You get the gist. "God is able. Whether he delivers us from the foe is up to him. As for us, we're sticking with God."

That's how faith operates. Faith does not look to success or to survival. Faith knows and trusts God. It defers to him. It submits to his will. Faith surrenders self to God. It says, "Come what may I will trust and obey."

Fortified Faith

Jehoshaphat went out against the foe. It had not shrunk in size. It was still a vast horde intent on harm. What had shrunk was his fear. The tumor of his fear had been reduced in size and potency by the chemotherapy of faith. That faith was made effective with the potency of God's truth. Fear had shriveled so that it no longer impeded going out against what God had brought.

In fact, God gives us trials that we might have opportunity to learn of him and to exercise our faith in him. That exercise makes faith stronger because God becomes bigger in our eyes. Like muscles that grow large against the opposition of weights in the gym, faith grows by the opposition trials present in our lives.

"Believe in the LORD your God . . . ; believe his prophets" (2 Chron. 20:20). Those words are more than a pep talk. Jehoshaphat was not prefiguring Knute Rockne as the

Fighting Irish prepared to do battle on the gridiron. Jehoshaphat was not spouting off pious sounding platitudes like the motivational speaker du jour. He was calling the people to faith. He was directing their sights to God as they headed out to confront the adversary.

To walk in faith is not to walk blindly, wishfully, or naively. It is not to venture out in quixotic idealism, minimizing or denying the severity of the trial in which we find ourselves. It is to walk with the clarity of spiritual sight.

Edvard Munch's *The Scream* has served any number of parodies. One that I saw that is particularly apt was a drawing of the painting in which the haunted figure was fitted with headphones. Isn't that often the way we handle life? We drown it out with diversion. Instead of even trying to deal with the surging tsunamis of life, we simply seek to cope by trying to avoid or deny or escape. Faith deals in reality, holding the assurance of things hoped for and the conviction of things not seen (Heb. 11:1).

He who has brought the crisis to us calls us to handle that crisis for his glory, by his means, toward his ends. And the remarkable thing is, in so doing, we can expect blessing.

10

Aftermath of Grace

That place has been called the Valley of Beracah.

On a note of praise, even in an atmosphere of worship, Jehoshaphat led his grossly overmatched, vastly outnumbered army out to take on the enemy. Instead of a battle cry, his soldiers sang and gave thanks to the Lord for his steadfast love. The battle was engaged, but it was the Lord who fought on their behalf. He caused the vast horde to implode, fighting with one another. "They all helped to destroy one another" (v. 23). Before the Lord, the enemy was routed.

It's almost as if the battle were a side note to the account. The lion's share of the detail is devoted to variegated prayer to God (i.e., praise, confession, thanksgiving, petition), and the giving of glory to God who fights on behalf of his people. A mere two verses are given to the description of the battle. Perhaps that's reflective of the power of the "vast horde" in comparison to the power of the Lord God Almighty. Perhaps the paucity of battle details is indicative of what God actually wants us to see in the account. Perhaps the presenting crisis is tangential to what is the real battle.

Field of Battle

When we face crisis in our lives and try to find voice in our times of distress, the main issue is not the crisis, although it's hard to convince ourselves of that at the time. When a mountain of debt or a devastating diagnosis or a ruptured relationship besieges us, it certainly seems the main issue. But is it?

Numerous times I have stood alongside men, women, couples, and families in the trenches of a battle they face. By prayer and God's revealed Word, we have traveled from the feebleness of fear to the fortress of faith in God their refuge and strength, an ever-present help in trouble. Yet, when the storm is past I find the same fears and "what ifs" and frustrations have crept back in. They have not been washed away by the tide of trouble. Many times those involved have even been inoculated by the episode, inviting a stronger strain of the disease of doubt, more resistant to change. They may have overcome the financial, physical, or whatever sort of tyranny confronted them, but they remain in the grip of a foe occupying their heart. The inner oppressor, silhouetted and exposed by the flashing of the bombs of the assault, continues to hold ground.

The primary front on which God works in our lives is the battleground of our hearts. The main issue, the heart of the matter, is the matter of the heart. Where are our hearts in respect to God? Who is greater in our eyes, God or the crisis? Whose will do we really want? How will we handle ourselves in the face of fear? These are the questions that occupy center stage in the wartime drama with Jehoshaphat.

The Spoils of Struggle

Growing up at the beach I witnessed many severe storms. Often during a hurricane or nor'easter I would walk down to the shore and take in the fury of the gray, white-capped, swelling, surging ocean. Sometimes the water would come all the way up, completely engulfing the beach, washing even over the boardwalk. It was an impressive sight.

When the storm passed and the waters receded, the beach would be littered with debris—a treasure trove of shells, driftwood, and sea life left behind by the retreating tide. Remarkably, the only way those treasures could be found on the beach was through the storm. The wind and the waves served as the vehicle through which the debris was deposited.

Storms come into our lives with the purpose of God, carrying the treasures of his providence, leaving an aftermath of his grace. We listen again to the wisdom of God as

Moses ministers God's Word to the people in their wilderness wanderings:

> And you shall remember the whole way that the LORD your God has led you these forty years in the wilderness, that he might humble you, testing you to know what was in your heart, whether you would keep his commandments or not. And he humbled you and let you hunger and fed you with manna, which you did not know, nor did your fathers know, that he might make you know that man does not live by bread alone, but man lives by every word that comes from the mouth of the LORD. Your clothing did not wear out on you and your foot did not swell these forty years. Know then in your heart that, as a man disciplines his son, the LORD your God disciplines you. (Deut. 8:2–5)

Moses describes God's hand in the deprivation for enrichment of his people. God is at work as a good and wise father in the lives of his children. Many times the storm is the only mode of transportation by which those blessings of his grace and fruit of his loving discipline could come.

James in the New Testament reminds us that the trials of our lives carry with them the purpose of God.

> Count it all joy, my brothers, when you meet trials of various kinds, for you know that the testing of your faith produces steadfastness. And let steadfastness have its full effect, that you may be perfect and complete, lacking in nothing. (James 1:2–4)

The joy is not in the trial per se, but in the personal hand of our God and Father who brings the trial to us and in the expectation of what that trial will bring to us in keeping with his perfect purpose.

God's intention is that the crises we face in our lives that cause us so much distress will work to make us stronger, more fully committed, better acquainted with the sufficiency of his grace, more determined to know and serve him, and more mature in Christlike character by his handiwork of grace. That's what James means when he speaks of us being "perfect and complete, lacking in nothing." He's not referring to our bank accounts but to the vault of heavenly riches that we will carry into eternity as he grows us for glory.

To the Victor

As was typical in battle in ancient times, to the victor belonged the spoils. In this case, Jehoshaphat's army reaped the spoils of the vicarious victory. Such was the extent of the booty that we are told, "they could carry no more." "They were three days in taking the spoil, it was so much" (2 Chron. 20:25).

They ventured into the field of battle to survey the aftermath of God's grace, to take what they had not earned and to gather up an abundance they had not expected. What an amazing picture of God's grace! That's what grace is. Grace gives us what we do not deserve. It comes to us as a gift—unmerited, unearned, unexpected. Their faith had not earned a blessing, but it certainly had received a blessing.

We might grimace to think of war and plundering the spoil, but that offers an apt picture for the aftermath of the crisis that has oppressed us. It reminds us that there is a struggle involved and blessing from our God, who is not merely waiting for us as *a* light at the end of the tunnel. He is with us as *the* light *in* the tunnel to guide and provide, brightening our way to the bounty of blessing carried by the trial that awaits our exploration.

Now weighed down with bounty instead of dread, Jehoshaphat and his victorious army assembled in the "Valley of Beracah" (v. 26). Beracah means "blessing." The concept cuts two ways. On the one hand it speaks to the blessing we receive, for which we are to scour the field of battle, the treasures of grace brought by our God to us through the upheaval. On the other hand, Beracah speaks to the blessings we are to give. We read as they assembled in that valley: "for there they blessed the LORD" (v. 26). We are to be both recipients and respondents. We are to take stock of what our God has brought us in the storm, and we are to take heed to express to our God glory and gratitude.

Gathering the Gain

Just as the seashore is strewn with treasures carried by the storm, so the crises of our lives bring to us the treasure trove of blessings from the hand of our God. Often in our relief to be done with the trial, we are eager to move on—quickly. But once the tide of turmoil has receded, we don't want to overlook returning to the sands of battle to collect the spoils. Just looking to surviving the tumult forgets the purpose of God in the storm and neglects the gleanings of grace deposited by it in our lives.

It is on the real field of battle that we must search to glean the spoils of war. If the primary target area of God in his bringing us to face the crisis is the heart, then it is to the heart we must direct our attention to scour the ground and gather the gain.

What are some of the blessings we might find after the high tide of crisis has withdrawn? We look to know God better. What has he taught us about himself? What do we now know more experientially and not just intellectually? We look to know ourselves better. What areas for spiritual growth has the trial exposed in our lives? What undesirable character qualities has the storm unearthed that we need to address to mature in Christlikeness?

In God's workmanship of grace, we are likely to find the fruits of joy, peace, patience. We measure ourselves against the doorjamb of spiritual maturity and discover we have grown in the grace and knowledge of our Lord Jesus Christ. Our God has raised us up with the high-water mark of his grace that has and will lead us through many dangers, toils, and snares.

As his children, God has used the hardship of the trial to train us and mold us in our spiritual growth. Trials often bring spiritual growth spurts. We have tested the strength of the everlasting arms of our God and found them sufficient.

We have tasted and seen that the Lord is good and experienced the blessing of those who have taken refuge in him. We find that our often-discordant hearts have been tuned to sing his praise and to find joy even in the midst of trial.

That the World May Know

Following their amazing victory, accomplished by the Lord on their behalf, the army of Jehoshaphat returned with joy, "for the LORD had made them rejoice over their enemies." And the glory of God became renowned.

That begs the question as we engage in trial or emerge from it, Who around us is within sight of God's working? Who is within earshot of our expressions of anguish, joy, gratitude and praise? For whom is the power and grace of our Lord God displayed in our distress that they might behold his working through us and give glory to our Father in heaven? Isn't that really the greatest goal—that the name of the Lord would be renowned and that glory redound to him, both by us and by others? Neighbors, friends, coworkers, family, and bystanders would see his working and say, 'What kind of God is this who does such great things and provides so remarkably for his children?'

Conclusion

About 11:30 at night, the phone rings. Your heart lodges in your throat. Your teenage son has never missed his 11:00 p.m. curfew. You've been pacing the floor wondering where he is. You pick up the phone and hear words that every parent dreads: "There's been an accident; could you come to the hospital right away?" You arrive to hear the details of the accident and to learn that your son is dead. How can you handle it?

> O our God, will you not execute judgment on them? For we are powerless against this great horde that is coming against us. We do not know what to do, but our eyes are on you.

The tests have come back. With somber face, the doctor sits opposite you. The tumor is malignant. Surgery is mandated. Prognosis grim.

> O our God, will you not execute judgment on them? For we are powerless against this great horde that is coming against us. We do not know what to do, but our eyes are on you.

She was your best friend. Now she can't even remember your name. Sometimes she doesn't even recognize you. Your mother who was always so intelligent and competent, a rock in your life, now shackled in the advanced stages of Alzheimer's. She looks like your mom, but your mom is not there.

> O our God, will you not execute judgment on them? For we are powerless against this great horde that is coming against us. We do not know what to do, but our eyes are on you.

Once again, you find yourself confessing to God the same sin. You had resolved to overcome it, to turn your back on it. You would not let yourself fall into it again. But here you are, disgusted with yourself, wondering how you will ever escape its clutches.

> O our God, will you not execute judgment on them? For we are powerless against this great horde that is coming against us. We do not know what to do, but our eyes are on you.

You never saw it coming. The possibility had never even occurred to you. But that morning your husband of thirteen years had told you that he wanted a divorce. The man with whom you shared your life, the father of your two children, the one with whom you intended to grow old together, leaving, rejecting. Never have you felt more stunned and empty and fearful.

> O our God, will you not execute judgment on them? For we are powerless against this great horde that is coming against us. We do not know what to do, but our eyes are on you.

It finally caught up with you. You knew it would. You have no one to blame but yourself. How many times had you resolved to cut up those credit cards? To cut back on your spending? To cut out the lifestyle of affluence? And now you look up to see yourself buried in such debt that you cannot even see the crest of its mountain.

> O our God, will you not execute judgment on them? For we are powerless against this great horde that is coming against us. We do not know what to do, but our eyes are on you.

You're the one who is supposed to lead, to be in charge. All eyes are on you. The team has just imploded, detonated by the explosives of volatile relationships, ignited by the short fuse of anger and impatience. It's a mess. How can you possibly lead? How will your boss react?

> O our God, will you not execute judgment on them? For we are powerless against this great horde that is coming against us. We do not know what to do, but our eyes are on you.

Finding Voice in Your Distress

What situation are you facing? What crisis looms over you making you feel small and helpless, where the endorphins of distress surge through your body causing your heart to sink and your knees to buckle? You don't know what to do. Don't know how to cope. Don't know what to pray. God gives you voice:

> O our God, will you not execute judgment on them? For we are powerless against this great horde that is coming against us. We do not know what to do, but our eyes are on you.

Or perhaps you could personalize it: "O my God, will you not intervene? I am powerless against this great adversity coming against me. I do not know what to do, but my eyes are on you."

God is greater than whatever you face. Call on him to act on your behalf, the Almighty doing what you cannot, the All-wise God doing what is best. Cast yourself upon him.

Strength in Weakness

Might I suggest that this prayer of Jehoshaphat anticipates for us the posture and pattern for the powerless reflected throughout Scripture in the relationship of God's people with him in the travails of life. As Peter would write under the inspiration of the same Spirit a thousand years later:

> Humble yourselves, therefore, under the mighty hand of God so that at the proper time he may exalt you, casting all your anxieties on him, because he cares for you. (1 Peter 5:6–7)

And Peter goes on to identify for us our *ultimate enemy*, and it's not physical, financial, or factional, but spiritual:

> Be sober-minded; be watchful. Your adversary the devil prowls around like a roaring lion, seeking someone to devour. Resist him, firm in your faith, knowing that the same kinds of suffering are being experienced by your brotherhood throughout the world. (1 Peter 5:8–9)

And our *ultimate hope.*

> And after you have suffered a little while, the God of all grace, who has called you to his eternal glory in Christ, will himself restore, confirm, strengthen, and establish you. To him be the dominion forever and ever. Amen. (1 Peter 5:10–11)

Deciding who the "foe" is that we call upon our God to judge will dictate and direct our prayer. The apostle Paul affirms, "For we do not wrestle against flesh and blood, but against the rulers, against the authorities, against the cosmic powers over this present darkness, against the spiritual forces of evil in the heavenly places" (Eph. 6:12). All the more do we see the urgency of taking refuge and finding strength in the Lord of hosts. It is against the ultimate foe that the call for God to judge falls with greatest force. It is with this spiritual adversary that the severest battle for the heart is fought.

It may be God's purpose to grant us relief in this life and, as with Job, restore our fortunes with the abundant interest of blessings. Or, God may design to grant us relief in the age to come, where:

> He will wipe away every tear from their eyes, and death shall be no more, neither shall there be mourning nor crying nor pain anymore, for the former things have passed away. (Rev. 21:4)

The Crisis and the Commonplace

We've made use of Jehoshaphat's prayer in respect to those *extraordinary* times of distress in our lives. As we see it in context of 2 Chronicles, it is one of those "break the glass and sound the alarm" kind of prayers. But it also finds a place in the ebb and flow of *ordinary* life. The salt pile used for negotiating the interstate when the blizzard hits is the same salt pile we tap for the icy patches on the sidewalk we will surely encounter in the pathways of our lives in what can be a cold and inhospitable world.

The prayer of Jehoshaphat fits in adopting the posture our God would have for us in the everydayness of life, the small dips and the deep valleys. We need the help of our God not only in the enormity, but also in the ordinary. In fact, that's one of the lessons he wants us to learn. And we need constant reminders, as we are inclined to the misalignment of self-sufficiency.

What's going on in your life right now? What has your stomach in knots? What's keeping you up at night, robbing you of much needed sleep? "God gave him rest all around" (2 Chron. 20:30). From panic to peace, God gave Jehoshaphat rest through his answer to Jehoshaphat's prayer.

Such is the fruit of prayer that seeks and serves the true and living God. The apostle Paul, captive in prison, highlights this principle of God's wisdom:

> Rejoice in the Lord always; again I will say, Rejoice. Let your reasonableness be known to everyone. The Lord is at hand; do not be anxious about anything, but in everything by prayer and supplication with thanksgiving let your requests be made known to God. And the peace of God, which surpasses all understanding, will guard your hearts and your minds in Christ Jesus. (Phil. 4:4–7)

In the ultimate battle we face in distress, the battle for the heart, we desperately need such a Guard, remembering our Lord is "at hand."

Seasoned With Supplication

There we have it. The prayer of Jehoshaphat. Is that where you would have expected a king, the commander of an army, to find strength? Many times I have prayed that prayer and used it as a pattern for my own crying out to

God. It seemed all I could muster. And it always fit, always had the right aftertaste, always held me until the help of my God arrived, always helped me to press on.

The prayer of Jehoshaphat is not a gimmick. Not a canned prayer to be recited as a mantra. It's more of an icebreaker prayer, a prayer that puts us on the right track to walking with our God in delight and dependence. It serves as a vehicle given by God to give voice to us in our fears, calling out to him whom we are to fear. It's like getting that first glob out of the ketchup bottle. It flows freely after that, a condiment to life that is often hard to swallow.

> O our God, will you not execute judgment on them? For we are powerless against this great horde that is coming against us. We do not know what to do, but our eyes are on you.

Climax

We have come to the end of the prayer but not to the end of the story. Our treatment of this prayer of Jehoshaphat would neither be complete nor true to the book in which it is found without one last word, the crescendo of the symphony of salvation. This prayer, the events that surround it, and the resolution it seeks have their ultimate end in Jesus Christ. The Bible is a redemptive document. The star of it is not Jehoshaphat. The great heroes of the faith are not Moses, Joseph, Gideon, David, John, Peter, or Paul. The hero is Jesus. The Bible speaks of God's wisdom, love, power, justice, and grace. All these are expressed in the person and work of Jesus Christ.

The New Testament book of Hebrews takes us from the Old Testament root and stem of God's pattern and promise to show us the unwilting, incomparable, glorious blossom of God's provision of grace in Jesus.

> Long ago, at many times and in many ways, God spoke to our fathers by the prophets, but in these last days he has spoken to us by his Son, whom he appointed the heir of all things, through whom also he created the world. He is the radiance of the glory of God and the exact imprint of his nature, and he upholds the universe by the word of his power. After making purification for sins, he sat down at the right hand of the Majesty on high. (Heb. 1:1–3)

In Jehoshaphat we have a picture, a preview, a fore-taste of God's salvation. We are without resources, without recourse, set by our sin on a course of ultimate distress and destruction. There is no one righteous, not even one. No one can stand before God and claim innocence.

The wrath of God abides on us. The juggernaut of the perfectly just judgment of a holy God looms before all of us. We cannot escape. We have no ability to defend ourselves. His wrath is the heat-seeking missile poised to be launched at the inflamed target of us as sinners.

But isn't God loving? Indeed he is, but not at the expense of his holiness. He cannot deny himself. As a holy God, he cannot leave sin unpunished. The love of God is a redemptive concept. It is a gracious love, an unexpected, undeserved, unmerited refuge of redemption. It is a love bound up in the person and work of Jesus Christ.

Listen to God as he displays this love and note the context for it.

> God shows his love for us in that while we were still sinners, Christ died for us. Since, therefore, we have now been justified by his blood, much more shall we be saved by him from the wrath of God. (Rom. 5:8–9)

John 3:16, perhaps the best-known, most quoted verse in the Bible, provides the same backdrop by which the love of God is demonstrated.

> For God so loved the world that he gave his only Son, that whoever believes in him should not perish but have eternal life.

The context in both of these New Testament passages that qualifies the glory of God's love is the escape of perishing before his justice. In case we misunderstand, John spells it out for us in the verses that follow.

> For God did not send his Son into the world to condemn the world, but in order that the world might be saved through him. Whoever believes in him is not condemned, but whoever does not believe is condemned already, because he has not believed in the name of the only Son of God. (John 3:17–18)

The fortress of God's love, the refuge of his mercy, the shelter of his grace is Jesus Christ. His work on the cross had to do with the collision of God's justice and love. It is in Christ that the justice of God's holiness and the love of his gracious goodness kiss one another, so that God "might be just and the justifier of the one who has faith in Jesus" (Rom. 3:26).

Jehoshaphat means, "the LORD has judged." The Jehoshaphat whose prayer we have explored was not able to face the foe. He was not the deliverer. Jesus, the ultimate Jehoshaphat, was able. He is the God who judges and God incarnate who was judged as he stood in the place of sinners. He is the One, the only one, able to deliver from the definitive crisis. It is in Christ and him crucified that God has judged, the wrath of his justice fully spent, and the guilt of sin atoned for. Our sin laid upon him, the wrath of the holy God that had to be discharged lest God be unjust is diverted from those to whom it was rightfully aimed to him who stretched out in love on the cross. In another biblical image, the cup of God's wrath placed in our hands as sinners is lovingly taken from us by Christ at the cross and drained to its very dregs, exhausted upon him who was without sin. In its place God gives the cup of blessing, blessings earned by Christ and received by faith (cf. Ps. 75:8; Matt. 26:39; 1 Cor. 10:16).

Jesus explains his deliverance for us:

> Truly, truly, I say to you, whoever hears my word and believes him who sent me has eternal life. He does not come into judgment, but has passed from death to life. (John 5:24)

That deliverance had to do with justice. With it is appended his promise of escape from the ultimate foe, to find life—new, abundant, and eternal—through faith in Christ.

Second Chronicles 20 gives us a beautiful representation of the gospel, where we admit we have nothing to commend ourselves to God. We are impotent to save ourselves from the gavel of God's justice and the sentence of condemnation that deservedly awaits us, more dreadful than any coalition man could muster. It is in that position of spiritual bankruptcy and impotency that we turn not away from God, but to him. We run to him. We cry out to him in our distress.

And he does not remain silent to our cries or callous to our need. The answer to which he points us is the Son of his love, his provision for our deepest need. And his promise is that all who turn to Jesus Christ in faith he will not turn away, but grant the promise, not merely of temporal rest all around as he gave to Jehoshaphat, but of eternal life and everlasting rest through his victory.

John Newton, the slave trader who became a slave to Christ, composer of "Amazing Grace," sums up the position God would have us take:

> No strength of our own and no goodness we claim;
> Yet, since we have known of the Savior's great name,
> In this our strong tower for safety we hide:
> The Lord is our power. The Lord will provide.

Indeed, the Lord has provided. That's the message of the Bible. Without that provision there would be no hope, nowhere to turn, no escape, no recourse. Without that provision, we would turn to God and find only silence as the foe of our sin advances against us. But praise God that he has given his Son in which God himself fought the foe. The victory is his and becomes ours by faith that rests in him.

May God pour out upon you a spirit of grace and supplication that you might grow in the knowledge of him and of his amazing love, power, and provision in Jesus Christ.

2 Chronicles 20:1–30 (ESV)

[1] After this the Moabites and Ammonites, and with them
some of the Meunites, came against Jehoshaphat for battle.
[2] Some men came and told Jehoshaphat, "A great multitude
is coming against you from Edom, from beyond the sea;
and, behold, they are in Hazazon-tamar" (that is, Engedi).
[3] Then Jehoshaphat was afraid and set his face to seek the
LORD, and proclaimed a fast throughout all Judah. [4] And
Judah assembled to seek help from the LORD; from all the
cities of Judah they came to seek the LORD.

[5] And Jehoshaphat stood in the assembly of Judah and
Jerusalem, in the house of the LORD, before the new court,
[6] and said, "O LORD, God of our fathers, are you not God
in heaven? You rule over all the kingdoms of the nations.
In your hand are power and might, so that none is able

to withstand you. 7 Did you not, our God, drive out the
inhabitants of this land before your people Israel, and
give it forever to the descendants of Abraham your friend?
8 And they have lived in it and have built for you in it a
sanctuary for your name, saying, 9 'If disaster comes upon
us, the sword, judgment, or pestilence, or famine, we will
stand before this house and before you—for your name is
in this house—and cry out to you in our affliction, and you
will hear and save.' 10 And now behold, the men of Ammon
and Moab and Mount Seir, whom you would not let Israel
invade when they came from the land of Egypt, and whom
they avoided and did not destroy—11 behold, they reward
us by coming to drive us out of your possession, which you
have given us to inherit. 12 O our God, will you not execute
judgment on them? For we are powerless against this great
horde that is coming against us. We do not know what to
do, but our eyes are on you."

13 Meanwhile all Judah stood before the LORD, with their
little ones, their wives, and their children. 14 And the Spirit
of the LORD came upon Jahaziel the son of Zechariah, son
of Benaiah, son of Jeiel, son of Mattaniah, a Levite of the
sons of Asaph, in the midst of the assembly. 15 And he said,
"Listen, all Judah and inhabitants of Jerusalem and King
Jehoshaphat: Thus says the LORD to you, 'Do not be afraid
and do not be dismayed at this great horde, for the battle
is not yours but God's. 16 Tomorrow go down against them.
Behold, they will come up by the ascent of Ziz. You will
find them at the end of the valley, east of the wilderness
of Jeruel. 17 You will not need to fight in this battle. Stand

firm, hold your position, and see the salvation of the LORD
on your behalf, O Judah and Jerusalem.' Do not be afraid
and do not be dismayed. Tomorrow go out against them,
and the LORD will be with you."

18 Then Jehoshaphat bowed his head with his face to
the ground, and all Judah and the inhabitants of Jerusalem
fell down before the LORD, worshiping the LORD. 19 And the
Levites, of the Kohathites and the Korahites, stood up to
praise the LORD, the God of Israel, with a very loud voice.

20 And they rose early in the morning and went
out into the wilderness of Tekoa. And when they went
out, Jehoshaphat stood and said, "Hear me, Judah and
inhabitants of Jerusalem! Believe in the LORD your God,
and you will be established; believe his prophets, and you
will succeed." 21 And when he had taken counsel with the
people, he appointed those who were to sing to the LORD
and praise him in holy attire, as they went before the army,
and say,

> "Give thanks to the LORD,
> for his steadfast love endures forever."

22 And when they began to sing and praise, the LORD
set an ambush against the men of Ammon, Moab, and
Mount Seir, who had come against Judah, so that they were
routed. 23 For the men of Ammon and Moab rose against
the inhabitants of Mount Seir, devoting them to destruction, and when they had made an end of the inhabitants
of Seir, they all helped to destroy one another.

24 When Judah came to the watchtower of the wilderness,
they looked toward the horde, and behold, there were dead
bodies lying on the ground; none had escaped. 25 When
Jehoshaphat and his people came to take their spoil, they
found among them, in great numbers, goods, clothing, and
precious things, which they took for themselves until they
could carry no more. They were three days in taking the
spoil, it was so much. 26 On the fourth day they assembled
in the Valley of Beracah, for there they blessed the LORD.
Therefore the name of that place has been called the Valley
of Beracah to this day. 27 Then they returned, every man
of Judah and Jerusalem, and Jehoshaphat at their head,
returning to Jerusalem with joy, for the LORD had made
them rejoice over their enemies. 28 They came to Jerusalem
with harps and lyres and trumpets, to the house of the
LORD. 29 And the fear of God came on all the kingdoms of
the countries when they heard that the LORD had fought
against the enemies of Israel. 30 So the realm of Jehoshaphat
was quiet, for his God gave him rest all around.

Study Guide

Introduction

1. How are we first introduced to Jehoshaphat in 2 Chronicles 17:1–6? How would you describe his heart? What is noteworthy about the extent of his allegiance to God?

2. Read 2 Chronicles 17:7–9 and 18:4–6. What was Jehoshaphat's attitude toward the Word of God? How does that attitude relate to the place God has in his heart?

3. Read 2 Chronicles 18:28–34. How is the amazing providence of the God to whom we pray evident in this account? What do we learn about the word of God?

4. Read 2 Chronicles 19:4–7. How did the character of God affect Jehoshaphat's view of life in what should be done and how things should be done?

5. As you read the heart of Jehoshaphat's prayer in 2 Chronicles 20:12, what is its initial appeal that draws you into it?

6. Why in the face of distress was it Jehoshaphat's reflex to pray?

7. Read the assessment of Jehoshaphat's life in 2 Chronicles 20:31–33. What is highlighted? What sort of legacy did Jehoshaphat leave?

Chapter 1: Storm Clouds on the Horizon

1. How would you describe the faithfulness of Jehoshaphat to God in 2 Chronicles 19:4–11? Why might the threat of 2 Chronicles 20:1 surprise us against this backdrop? What does this say about the distress God allows into our lives?

2. Why is distress something we should expect in this world? How does God use trials and troubles in our lives? What perspective and encouragement does Jesus give us in the face of distress? See John 16:33; 14:27.

3. Read 2 Chronicles 20:1–2. How would you describe the forces coming against Jehoshaphat from this brief setting? How is the immanence and momentum of the threat communicated?

4. Jehoshaphat's threat was a vast army. It appeared on the horizon unannounced and unprovoked. What sort of threat do you face in your life? Try to describe it in words. What exactly does it threaten?

5. Why does God turn our attention to Jehoshaphat and his response to the threat, rather than drawing us into the threat itself for a more detailed understanding? In

the threats of your life why would God have you turn your attention to yourself and your response? See Deuteronomy 8:2.

6. As we face distress in our lives, what does it mean for us to act and not merely react? How can distress rule and enslave us?

7. What is the difference between coping and hoping? What does hope bring to our handling of adversity that just tolerating or weathering adversity does not?

Chapter 2: Seeing beyond the Storm

1. Read 2 Chronicles 20:3–4. What was Jehoshaphat's reaction? How can fear mobilize or immobilize us in the face of severe distress?

2. In the range of human reactions, how else might this sentence have been completed: "Then Jehoshaphat was afraid and __________"? Why do you think the sentence in Jehoshaphat's case was completed, " . . . and set his face to seek the LORD"?

3. How can the storm clouds of distress in our lives obscure our view of God? What enables us to see beyond those clouds to find our focus and gain our bearings?

4. In the face of distress in our lives, what does it mean to "seek" the Lord? How does Psalm 46 direct us in seeking the Lord in such times?

5. Jehoshaphat "set his face" to seek the Lord. What does that expression convey? What does it entail? How does Jesus set his face in Luke 9:51–53? Why is setting our face important for the direction, stability, and goals in handling that distress?

6. What is fasting? What role did it not play in Jehoshaphat's dealing with the crisis? What role did it play? What in your life hinders your ability to see God through the storm for which you need to sharpen the visual acuity of your faith?

7. How does communion with God, dependence upon him, and trust in him in the smooth seas of life relate to seeking him in the storm-tossed seas of distress? How can your distresses provide occasions to know God better?

Chapter 3: Sharpening Our Gaze on Glory

1. Read 2 Chronicles 20:5–7. Why do you suppose Jehoshaphat led in public prayer instead of retreating to his prayer closet?

2. How would you define prayer? What value does prayer have in God's design for it?

3. Why is it important that we gain a clear focus on the One to whom we are praying and not just rush to cry for help? How does Jehoshaphat gain this focus?

4. What is the God like to whom you pray? Where do you get your ideas of what he is like? What ideas did the

philosophers in Acts 17:20–34 have about God? How is Paul able to make the correctives he does?

5. How do the descriptions of God employed by Jehoshaphat relate to the threat he faced? What descriptions of God can you mine from his Word that relate to your distress? As you take them to your lips, how do they drive you more deeply and confidently into the arms of God?

6. In verse 7 Jehoshaphat recounts how God came to the aid of his people in the past. What bearing would that have on the distress at hand? How have God's faithfulness and care been in evidence in your past, and how would that relate to your present?

7. Prayer involves not only petition but seeing and knowing God aright, even working to grow us in that knowledge. How is a greater knowledge of God evident in these passages: John 17:3; Ephesians 1:17; Colossians 1:10? How does the knowledge of God in Job 38–41 affect Job in his distress in Job 40:3–5 and 42:1–6?

Chapter 4: Privileged Access

1. Read 2 Chronicles 20:8–9. To what "house" is Jehoshaphat referring that God affixes the promise of access and responsiveness?

2. Read 2 Chronicles 6:1–42. What does the temple before which Jehoshaphat prays signify about God and his relationship with his people? What promises does God

make in reference to the temple that Jehoshaphat is now claiming in prayer?

3. What key of access do we find in Isaiah 41:8–9 for the promise of Isaiah 41:10?
4. Is there a physical temple today that speaks of God's presence among his people? See John 1:1, 14; Matthew 1:18–23. Do we need to go a particular place or wait for a particular time in order to pray?
5. What means does God provide for entering his presence? See 1 Timothy 2:5–6; Hebrews 4:14–16.
6. What right do we have to come before God? See Hebrews 10:1–22; Galatians 4:4–5; Matthew 7:7–11.
7. What attitude does God want of us as we would come before him in our need? See 2 Chronicles 7:12–16; Matthew 6:10; 26:42.

Chapter 5: Prevailing Prayer

1. Read 2 Chronicles 20:12. What is Jehoshaphat's actual petition in this prayer? For what things is he asking as he cries out for God's judgment?
2. Read 2 Chronicles 20:10–11. How does Jehoshaphat's request for God to judge apply to the crisis he faces at the moment? How might this request be expressed in the distress we face?

3. What three expressions qualify Jehoshaphat's petition in v. 12? What does each one mean? How would each one apply to us in our time of distress?

4. How does Paul's prayer in 2 Corinthians 12:7–10 parallel Jehoshaphat's prayer? What does this suggest about God's purpose in exposing our weakness, frailty, and helplessness in the distresses we face? What do you think God might be exposing in your own heart that would limit your awe of and dependence on him?

5. What does it mean to look to God in our strength and not only in our weakness, to seek him as our ability and not merely to augment it? How is this seen in the metaphor used by Jesus for our fruitfulness? See John 15:1–5.

6. In facing the distress we do, how does a posture of humility lead us to plead ignorance as well as impotence? How is this worked out in Isaiah 40:25–31?

7. In what way can we see God's goal in all this to be a display of his glory, his grace, and his goodness? How is this expressed in 1 Peter 5:5b–11?

Chapter 6: Sand Bags of Promise

1. Read 2 Chronicles 20:13–14. God directs our attention from Jehoshaphat's prayer in v. 12 to the people whom

he led in prayer in v. 13. Jehoshaphat's leadership affects those in his charge. How would your distress and the way you handle it affect others?

2. What posture should we adopt when we pray as we stand before God, our prayer having been lifted up to him? See Psalm 5:1–3. What keeps us from adopting that posture?

3. As we wait upon the Lord in prayer, what does it mean to submit our wills to his? Read Romans 11:33–36. How does Paul's declaration of praise on the heels of his discussion of God's mysterious will relate to our submitting our wills to God when we pray?

4. What does the expression "the Spirit of the LORD came upon" signify in 2 Chronicles 20:14? See 2 Chronicles 15:1; 18:23. Where does the Spirit speak to us that we might know the will of God? See 2 Timothy 3:16–17; 2 Peter 1:19–21.

5. How does God's written Word, the Bible, anchor you, shore you up, and buoy your spirits in the midst of distress? How can you bring that Word to bear so that the Spirit of God might minister to you in these ways?

6. What answer does God bring to Jehoshaphat's prayer in 2 Chronicles 20:15? Why would the prophet begin on the note of "listen"? What problems listening might we have in the thick of distress?

Chapter 7: Standing Firm

1. What reasons does God affix to his exhortation not to fear or be dismayed in 2 Chronicles 20:15? How does God dwarf and tame the threat that seems so huge to us? Fill in the blanks in dealing with the distress of your life: "I will not fear or be dismayed in the face of __________ because God ______________."

2. Look at the following passages of Scripture and identify 1) God's call and 2) God's "because": Psalm 23:1; 46:1–2; 62:8; Matthew 6:25–32.

3. When God calls us to "stand firm" in the tumult of our distress, what is he telling us? Look at these other passages where we are called to "stand firm" and pull together a picture of what is involved: Exodus 14:13–14; 1 Corinthians 16:13; Ephesians 6:13; 1 Peter 5:6–12.

4. Where do you try to find your footing in the face of your distress? One of the images God gives us of himself in his Word is our "Rock." (See Deut. 32:4; 2 Sam. 22:2–4; Ps. 18:2, 31, 46; Ps. 94:22; Isa. 26:4.) What does this metaphor communicate to us?

5. How can we position ourselves on this firm foundation? See Psalm 40:1–4; Matthew 7:24–27; 2 Corinthians 1:21–23.

6. Hebrews 12 speaks of weak knees and uneven paths in v. 12, looking both to us and to our circumstance. How

does God minister to us so that we can run the race he lays out for us in v. 1?

Chapter 8: Stepping Out

1. How do we reconcile God's assurances to Jehoshaphat in 2 Chronicles 20:15 that "the battle is not yours but God's" and in 2 Chronicles 20:17 that Jehoshaphat will not need to fight this battle with God's call in 2 Chronicles 20:16 for Jehoshaphat to "go down against" the enemy?

2. What truth is bound up in the expression "let go and let God"? What necessary balance, however, do we find here with Jehoshaphat and in passages such as Nehemiah 4:9 and 1 Peter 4:19 in our dealing with distress?

3. What relationship do we find between our activity and God's as we approach the trials and troubles of our lives? See John 15:5; Philippians 4:12–13.

4. What promises in 2 Chron 20:17 does God give Jehoshaphat as he calls him to step out against the formidable foe? How would those promises serve to embolden him, especially against the "fear" and "dismay" God mentions?

5. Why do you think Jehoshaphat's response is one of worship in 2 Chronicles 20:18–19? How can worship transform both our circumstance and our dealing with it? What does it mean to handle your situation of distress for God's glory? How does that affect your goals?

6. As you look at the distress of your life right now, what are you able to do about it? What might you pray to God in view of the fears that make your heart race at the very thought of taking action?

7. What are the "today" and "tomorrow" principles found in Matthew 6:33–34? As you look to deal with your distress, what can you put in the "today" category right now? What might go in the "tomorrow" category?

Chapter 9: Courage of Faith

1. Read 2 Chronicles 20:20–21. What does it suggest that Jehoshaphat went out to face the foe first thing in the morning? How is this also seen in Genesis 22:1–3? How does this relate to the faith of both men prominent in these passages?

2. How does Jehoshaphat encourage his troops? How do his words fortify their faith? To what does Jehoshaphat link success?

3. How does this call for faith relate to Jehoshaphat's prayer in 2 Chronicles 20:12? What words would faith that focuses on God speak into your distress?

4. Jehoshaphat tells the people to believe not only in the Lord their God but in his prophets. Why would he mention both as a basis for faith?

5. How does God define faith in Hebrews 11:1? What vantage point does faith give us for handling the distress

and ourselves in its onslaught? How can such faith fuel courage and confidence for pressing on?

6. Read Daniel 3:16–18. How is faith expressed here? How would such faith define success? How is such faith different from starry-eyed idealism? How is such faith legitimately optimistic? See Romans 8:18, 28–32.

7. How is unbelief obscuring your view of God and his Word? Of what might you say, "I do believe; help me in my unbelief"? How will you fortify your faith?

Chapter 10: Aftermath of Grace

1. Read the account of the battle in 2 Chronicles 20:22–23. Why do you think so little detail is recorded of the actual battle between Jehoshaphat and the enemy coalition?

2. What is remarkable and unexpected in the battle? How does this relate to God's promises in 2 Chronicles 20:15, 17? How does this relate to Jehoshaphat's obedience of faith in 2 Chronicles 20:16? What does this say about our casting our cares upon our God? See Ephesians 3:20.

3. What perspective on hardship does God give us in Deuteronomy 8:2–5? Why do you suppose trials are the furnace in which our faith is forged? How do trials prompt growth spurts in us?

4. How is the aftermath of God's grace evident in 2 Chronicles 20:24–26? Why would we call the spoils "grace"? What is grace?

5. What does "Beracah" mean? What blessings are in evidence in this passage? What does it mean to be blessed? What does it mean to bless the Lord? How do such psalms as Psalm 103 and Psalm 145 aid us in blessing the Lord?

6. Why is it important for us after making it through storms of distress to take stock of how God used that distress in our lives? Why would we expect to find anything, as we would take stock?

7. In what way is the heart the real field of battle? Use the searchlight of Psalm 139:23–24 and explore what areas the storms of your life have exposed in your heart for addressing in your growth in Christlikenesss. What blessings have you found left by the storm in your knowledge of God and his grace in your life? How can we see this dynamic in James 1:2–4?

8. Read 2 Chronicles 20:27–30. What was the response to God's mighty victory on their behalf? What were the repercussions for the surrounding nations?

Conclusion

1. What posture and pattern does the prayer of Jehoshaphat provide us in our powerlessness? In what way has it impressed you for finding voice in times of distress?

2. What danger is there in using 2 Chronicles 20:12 as a rote prayer? See Jesus' teaching on prayer in Matthew

6:5–13. How is this prayer in v. 12 more an icebreaker prayer or door of entry to the whole flow of 2 Chronicles 20:1–30?

3. How is Jehoshaphat's prayer useful for the ebb and flow of ordinary life as well as those times of great upheaval?
4. Who or what is our ultimate enemy in the face of distress for which we seek the intervention, power, and protection of our God? How is this enemy and God's blessing seen in these passages: Ephesians 6:10–18; 1 Peter 5:8–11?
5. God gave Jehoshaphat "rest all around." How is this reflected in Psalm 4 as a pattern for prayer in our distress?
6. How does our study of Jehoshaphat's prayer help us to make sense of Paul's writing from prison yet calling for rejoicing in Philippians 4:4–9?
7. What distress are you facing right now? Take it to God using the workstations of each of the previous chapters, making your answers above specific to your need. You might pull alongside a hurting friend and lead him or her from the storm clouds to the Valley of Beracah to help that person gather God's blessings.

Climax

1. Why is the end of the prayer of Jehoshaphat not the end of the story? See Luke 24:44–47; Romans 15:4; 1 Corinthians 10:11–13; Hebrews 11:1–12:3.

2. In what way does God give us in Jehoshaphat a preview and foreshadowing of his salvation in Jesus Christ?

3. Jehoshaphat's name means "the LORD has judged." Is God a God of judgment? See Exodus 34:4–7; Acts 17:30–31; Romans 1:18–20; Hebrews 9:27. Is God a God of love? See 1 John 4:13–19.

4. How is God's love displayed against the backdrop of his justice? See John 3:15–18; Romans 5:8–9.

5. How is Jesus the ultimate Jehoshaphat, the one where the Lord has judged? See Isaiah 53:1–12; John 19:17–30; Titus 3:3–7; 1 Peter 2:24–25.

6. In what way are the expressions, "the battle is not yours but God's," and "stand firm, hold your position and see the salvation of the LORD on your behalf" most gloriously realized in the cross of Christ? See Romans 3:10–26.

7. To what faith does Jehoshaphat point? See John 3:36; Ephesians 2:1–10. On what ground does saving faith rest? See 1 Corinthians 2:1–5; 15:12–20.

8. What are the ultimate blessings in view? See Ephesians 1:3–14; 2 Corinthians 1:19–21.

9. How can the prayer of Jehoshaphat in 2 Chronicles 20:12 be a prayer of repentance, cry for mercy, and expression of trust in God alone to save from the greatest foe—his righteous wrath on us as sinners? See Matthew 10:28.

In memoriam, J. Alan Groves (1952–2007),
having passed through the temporal
Valley of Baca to the eternal Valley of Berecah—
with Jesus. Blessings. SDG.

Stanley D. Gale has been married to his wife, Linda, since 1975. They have four children. He holds Bachelor of Arts and Master of Education degrees from the University of Delaware, a Master of Divinity degree from Westminster Theological Seminary in Philadelphia, and a Doctor of Ministry degree from Covenant Theological Seminary in St. Louis. He is an ordained pastor in the Presbyterian Church in America and has served his current charge in West Chester, Pennsylvania, since 1988. He is also the author of *Community Houses of Prayer: Reaching Others for Christ through Strategic Prayer* (Deo Volente Publishing) and *Warfare Witness: Contending with Spiritual Opposition in Everyday Evangelism* (Christian Focus Publications). He can be contacted through www.CHOPministry.net.